Skill
Size
Strength
& *Speed*

1986-87
BGSU Falcon Hockey Team

Interviews by Helen Rose Marketti

Skill, Size, Strength & Speed
Copyright ©2025 Helen Rose Marketti

All rights reserved. Blue Jade Press, LLC retains the right to reprint this book. Permission to reprint interviews from this collection must be obtained by the author.

ISBN- 978-1-961043-09-1

Published by:

Blue Jade Press, LLC

Blue Jade Press, LLC
Vineland, NJ 08360
www.bluejadepress.com

Introduction

Each and every time my "BG friends" and I have gotten together over the years, our reminiscing eventually found its way to the ice arena, the hockey games, the players, standing outside on game day and rushing to secure our tickets first thing on Monday mornings.

I remember the first hockey game I attended. My roommate and close friend, LeeAnn and I went with her cousin, Eric who had extra tickets. As the game got underway, it didn't take long for "crunch", "bang" and "crack" against the boards which made for an exciting sport to watch and we were hockey fans for life. There was always something happening on the ice. We loved it.

We purchased our "All Sports Pass" but primarily used it for hockey tickets! Our favorite area to sit was Section F, which was closer to the BG hockey bench at the time. Plus, it was also the area where the band played. It was an ideal surrounding.

At the time, when you're "living it", you're not thinking much about it. It was like second nature. Being supportive fans, being with our friends and sitting with the rest of the Bowling Green student body and community was the weekend staple for both Friday and Saturday nights. It was like sitting with an extended family. When the games were out of town, we listened on the radio and eagerly waited for our favorite players to be mentioned.

On Saturday, February 21, 1987, the Bowling Green hockey team won the CCHA title! I can still hear the crowd, the final buzzer and the celebrating pandemonium afterwards! Seeing the players piling on top of each other, and then skating around the arena carrying the championship banner still brings goosebumps and maybe a small tear or two. All of us in our early twenties at the time, proud to be a BGSU student, proud of our hockey team and witnessing the championship was an amazing experience!

Co-captains, Todd Flichel and Iain Duncan carried the championship banner first then handed it off to the rest of the team to share in the celebration. The players carried the banner to each of the four student sections so the fans could celebrate and share in the joy. I remember Marc Potvin was the first player to carry the banner over to our section. I can still see him plain as day.

I was so happy for the team, the coaches and for all of us. I was clapping so hard, I had bruising on the inside of my hands. I was screaming so loud, I had laryngitis for a few days. It was all worth every ounce of energy! We eagerly waited for the BG News (campus newspaper) so we could save the articles and photos.

Fast forward the reminiscing continued, my friend Beth mentioned how fun and special it would be if that time frame was captured in writing and suggested maybe I could take on that project since I am "the writer" of the group.

After thinking about that idea for a while, I decided to reach out to former head coach, Jerry York first to let him know about this idea. Thankfully, he was supportive and onboard. Gradually, I started reaching out to former players and support staff via social media. Thank you to my friend, Beth Ann Burkett for planting the seed for this book!

I have to give special thanks to Scott Paluch. Scott and I were in touch often as this project was gaining momentum and he was instrumental in assisting with contacting former players. If he wasn't directly in touch with someone, he knew someone else who was and gradually I found nearly everyone to complete this project.

I would like to thank Ray Schneider (*Cavallini from Kane*, 2015) for his encouragement, advice and support along this journey.

I would also like to thank Iain Duncan for his time and assistance.

I am grateful for everyone who participated. It was fun to share experiences and memories for a special time in our lives. Thank you to everyone. You made this book possible!

There are wonderful memories shared about Terry Flanagan, Marc Potvin, Greg Parks, Don Woods and Mark Pape.

Mark Pape owned Mark's Pizza Pub which we all referred to as, "Mark's". He provided a safe place for players and fans to gather relax and have conversation. It was an atmosphere similar to the television show, CHEERS, where everybody knew your name.

As you read these pages, you will feel the memories and the experiences from the coaches, players, mascots, referees, fans, support staff and more!

The 1986-87 hockey team was on fire! They deserve the recognition and attention. It was a special time in Bowling Green's hockey history. We lived it. We were there.

AY ZIGGY ZOOMBA
BGSU

~Helen Rose Marketti

"Looking back over fifty seasons of coaching college hockey, I vividly recollect some unique teams. Helen Marketti has captured one of these in the 1986-87 BGSU hockey team. This must read book is a fascinating look behind the scenes of a college season. All hockey fans can now share the incredible journey, cherished by all involved."

Jerry York, 2024

"In the summer of 1982, I arrived at Bowling Green State University as their new assistant hockey coach. It didn't take long to realize that there were some real good players and high expectations. Two years later, we won the national championship (1984) and now the bar was set. The team's goals would be league titles and championships.

The 1986-1987 team set out to achieve these same types of goals. We had an All-American goalie, a solid defense corps and an excellent group of forwards that could score and score again! We arguably had three of the best centermen in college hockey. If you wanted to play a skating game, we could skate. If you wanted to play physical, we could hit with the best of them. The team had a great second half run that that led to the CCHA title. The playoffs were not as kind with a tough overtime loss to Michigan State for the CCHA finals and then a defeat at Harvard in the NCAA tournament.

Overall, it was a great season that featured a team of character and characters. Great leadership came from the captains and seniors. A league title and 33 wins are solid achievements and not to be taken lightly.

It was a fun team to coach and be a part of both on and off the ice."

Buddy Powers, 2024

This book is dedicated in memory of
Terry Flanagan (Assistant Coach)
Marc Potvin (#14, Right Wing)
Greg Parks (#15, Center)

Their devotion, focus and motivation during their years at Bowling Green State University helped to build a strong hockey culture that resonates to this day with each new player that wears a Falcon Hockey jersey.

Throughout this book, there are many reminiscent thoughts about these three remarkable men as a coach, player, teammate, and friend.

Terry Flanagan

Marc Potvin

Greg Parks

Compliments of...

1986-87 BOWLING GREEN FALCONS

Front row (left to right): Head Coach Jerry York, Paul Ysebaert, Rob Urban, Tom Pratt, Iain Duncan, Gary Kruzich, Todd Flichel, Mike Natyshak, Brent Regan, Brian McKee, Assistant Coach Buddy Powers. Second row: Assistant Coach Terry Flanagan, Graduate Assistant Kevin Mann, Mark Lori, Geoff Williams, Steve Dickinson, Don Barber, Scott Paluch, Alan Leggett, Clarke Pineo, Andy Gribble, Brian Meharry, Assistant Coach Wayne Wilson, Team Physician Dr. Tom Wojciechowski. Third row: Head Trainer Bill Jones, Student Trainer Terry Slattery, Paul Connell, Nelson Emerson, Thad Rusiecki, Kevin Dahl, Marc Potvin, Joe Quinn, Chad Arthur, Greg Parks, Dan Kwilas, Equipment Manager Don Woods, Student Manager Jim Sibeto.

Table of Contents

Coaching Staff
Jerry York, *Head Coach*   2
Buddy Powers, *Assistant Coach*   5
Wayne Wilson, *Assistant Coach*   9
Kevin Mann, *Graduate Assistant*   12

Players
Paul Connell, *#1 Goalie*   16
Tom Pratt, *#2 Defenseman*   22
Todd Flichel, *Co-Captain #3 Defenseman*   26
Scott Paluch, *#4 Defenseman*   31
Kevin Dahl, *#5 Defenseman*   35
Thad Rusiecki, *#6 Defenseman*   39
Brian McKee, *#7 Defenseman*   43
Alan Leggett, *#8 Defenseman*   47
Rob Urban, *#10 Forward*   51
Paul Ysebaert, *#11 Center*   57
Mark Lori, *#12 Right Wing*   61
Andy Gribble, *#13 Right Wing*   65
Mark Potvin, *#14 Right Wing*   69
Greg Parks, *#15 Center*   72
Don Barber, *#16 Left Wing*   76
Geoff Williams, *#17, Forward*   77
Brent Regan, *#18 Defenseman*   78
Nelson Emerson *#19, Center*   82
Joe Quinn *#20, Right Wing*   87
Clarke Pineo *#21, Left Wing*   92
Brian Meharry *#22, Center*   96
Chad Arthur *#23, Left Wing*   101
Iain Duncan *Co-Captain #24 Left Wing*   105
Steve Dickinson *#26, Forward*   110
Mike Natyshak *#27, Right Wing*   114
Dan Kwilas *#29, Goalie*   119
Gary Kruzich *#35, Goalie*   120

Team Support
Scott Slater, *Family Ice Arena* 126
Ray Schneider, *Professor* 127
Doc Wojo (Dr. Tom Wojciechowski), *Team Doctor* 128
Jeff Weiss, *Statistician* 130
Angela Gorgone Swartz, *Statistician* 131
Don "Woody" Woods, *Equipment Manager* 133
Rob Schaad, *Student Equipment Manager* 137
Jeff Shell, *Referee* 139
Dennis Parish, *Referee* 142
Jim Sibeto, *Student Equipment Manager* 143
Rhonda Albers, *Frieda Falcon* 144
Janice Schriner, *Frieda Falcon* 148
Dave Shilling, *Freddie Falcon* 149
Dave Kuhar, *Freddie Falcon* 151
Tom Glick, *Announcer* 153
Scot Bressler, *Assistant in Athletic Business Affairs* 154
Todd Parker, *Friend/Fan* 155
Gene Hicks, *Friend/Fan* 157
Beth Burkett, *Friend/Fan* 159
LeeAnn Rasey *Friend/Fan* 161
Bruce Kratt, *Friend/Fan* 162

From the Photo Album 165
Photo Index 183

Coaching Staff

Jerry York and Terry Flanagan

Jerry York, Falcon Hockey Head Coach

Jerry York, Falcon Hockey Head Coach

Jerry York's reputation as a coach for collegiate hockey is pristine with wins, championships, awards and numerous accolades during his 15 years at Bowling Green State University. One of those memorable wins includes the 1984 NCAA Championship. His coaching career spans 50 years!

When I was growing up, there really wasn't any local teams that were playing. We just went down to the local frozen pond to play. I remember during the winter season; firemen would water down the tennis courts and turn them into ice rinks. I was actually more into baseball at the time to be honest. Then during high school, I shifted my interest from baseball to hockey. Hockey then became my primary sport.

I enjoyed watching Hockey Night in Canada and particularly followed the skills of Johnny Bucyk who had played for the Boston Bruins. I thought he was a great, solid player and he scored offensive goals. Bronco Horvath was another player I liked to watch. During my own career, I primarily played center. Sometimes a forward or wing but mostly center.

I feel hockey combines the physical contact of football and the brainwork to see what's ahead of you like basketball or soccer. If you stop to think about it, we're doing it all on artificial legs (skates) which makes the sport that much harder. The game requires skill and finesse but also hard-nosed combat.

When recruiting players, you are looking for their hockey skills, of course. But, you are also looking to see if the player will be a good fit for Bowling Green. For the most part, I thought we did a great job of bringing the right group of players to Bowling Green.

My coaching style was a combination of all the coaches that I ever played for. I always wanted to be fair and honest with the players. The team as a whole comes first. I always wanted each of them to give their all at practice because that is where we are going to get better. They were Falcons and it was important. I wanted them to be good examples, support the other sports teams at Bowling Green because they were representing the hockey team and the university. We built upon it each day, chapter-by-chapter, day by day, month by month. I woke up every day with gratitude that I was able to coach young players whether it was at Bowling Green or Boston College. I always felt challenged. I was never bored. It was a pleasure to work alongside the other coaches.

The players are the ones who chose Todd Flichel and Iain Duncan to be their captains. They were leaders. They were respected and both of them did a terrific job for the team and for Bowling Green. They were both critical to our championship. (CCHA, 1987) Winning that night was an ecstatic feeling, definitely a great evening.

I knew Terry Flanagan, when he played in New Hampshire. His father ran a hockey program in Stratford. Terry was an unbelievable person for BG Hockey and the community. It was a pleasure just to have him in our lives. I remember we were driving back from a recruiting trip from Toronto. He pulled the car over and asked if I could drive the rest of the way. He said he did not feel well and his vision was getting blurry. The next day he went to the doctor, which led to the discovery of his brain tumor. It was a very difficult time for all of us. He was a quality person. His coaching style was hands on. Everyone respected and loved him.

Marc Potvin, came out of Stratford as well. The team, the community and coaching staff, loved him. Life takes its twists and turns. I was stunned to hear the news when he passed away.

Greg Parks, was one of my favorite players. He worked hard. He was tenacious with the puck. For a smaller player, he never took any guff. He had great skill.

For new hockey players, be sure to enjoy the whole experience of attending Bowling Green, which is a remarkable university from academics to athletics. Learn the history of the town and meet as many fellow students as you can. Be your best possible self and make a positive impact on those around you.

Buddy Powers, Assistant Coach

Buddy Powers, Assistant Coach

I grew up in Boston and I was always a Bruins fan. When I was a teenager, Bobby Orr (Boston Bruins) came along and I think he made hundreds of kids in Boston want to play hockey.

I played hockey at Boston University. I remember thinking that college hockey was pretty cool. I thought that maybe I could be involved with it in some way for the rest of my life. I was interested in coaching and started my coaching career at Colgate University. By way of conversations and connections, I was interviewed by Jerry York for the assistant coaching position at Bowling Green State University. That was in 1982. I'm very lucky that he picked me to be his assistant. I was at Bowling Green as an assistant coach for six years. (1982-1988)

At the time, my role was more of "bad cop" and Jerry was the "good cop". I had worked with other coaches who were very intense and direct. Jerry had a different style of coaching. He was always looking at the positive side of things. He dug in and went to work. Watching Jerry coach and working alongside him not only helped me as a coach but also as a human being. Jerry saw the positive side of things most of the time and I feel that rubbed off on the players. They could play at ease and not be uptight. It gave the guys the best chance to put their best foot forward. Jerry had expectations, rules and so forth. It was a discipline and everyone needed to follow it.

When recruiting for Bowling Green we thought we could pretty much go head-to-head with most of the other teams to recruit players. We would win our share of battles and lose our share of battles. To simplify, we looked for players who had skill, size, strength and speed. And, if you had a cross over with a player who possessed more than one of these traits then you had yourself a bona fide, big-time talent. If you look back on the roster for the 86-87 team, we had all of those traits represented. If you wanted to play up and down the ice, we could do that. If you wanted to muck it up and bang around, we could do that with the best of them as well.

A good hockey player has good character, skill sense, handles the puck well and has good skating ability. They need to have hockey sense, which is a big factor. It makes them the player that they are. You can always work on getting a player stronger but difficult to get them smarter.

Game nights were always an adrenaline rush. Every game takes on a life of its own. The atmosphere before a game was fabulous. We packed the place for every game. It was a rough place to play if you were the visiting team.

Our co-captains were Todd Flichel and Iain Duncan. Todd was more of the silent type, led by example and had a positive influence. Iain was more vocal and physical. It was hard for anyone not to follow him.

When you win a championship, you have to remember that you got there by a culmination of games. It's a short season and it is over before you realize it. During those years at Bowling Green, we always had the reputation of being a good team during regular season. We had depth and quality. It was an outstanding line up. We had the formula for success with that roster and scored a lot of goals.

When I first came to Bowling Green, Terry Flanagan was the graduate assistant. We got an apartment together. We spent a lot of time together and became close friends. Our lives were intertwined. It was a devastating time when we found out he had cancer.

When you are in the Slater Ice Arena and look up towards the press box, there is a photo of Terry and Jerry. Even now, when I go out onto the ice, I look up at that photo and always say, "Hi Terry." He was one of the greatest guys that I ever met in my life.

Marc Potvin was one of our heavy weight guys. You wanted checks to be finished and he did exactly that. He was a great teammate in the locker room and on the ice.

Greg Parks was one of my favorites. He wasn't a big guy but he played with a lot of grit and a lot of skill. When we got him to commit to play at Bowling Green, we were ecstatic. Greg never wanted to take a backseat to anyone. He always wanted to show what he could do.

My advice to hockey players is to remember the game. Try to have fun. You need to enjoy the game. Hockey is hard. It's a hard and physical sport. It's a sport that you need to fall in love with to get the most out of it. Whoever is able to find that feeling and puts something into it, will then get something out of it.

Wayne Wilson, Assistant Coach

Wayne Wilson, Assistant Coach

I was playing hockey in Guelph, Ontario and knew that George McPhee and Brian MacLellan were playing at Bowling Green. They were from Guelph, as well. I never had heard of Bowling Green until George and Brian started playing there. One thing led to another and eventually Coach Jerry York and Bill Wilkinson who was an assistant coach at the time brought me to BG.

I fell in love with Bowling Green. I thought the hockey program was unbelievably strong. It was exciting to be there. I played at Bowling Green from 1980 to 1984. To be honest, I was hoping to turn pro and play in Europe but those plans fell through. So, I first became a graduate assistant for the hockey team and then moved into the position as an assistant coach.

I think the excitement of BG hockey fans is what made the environment. They were boisterous and fun. Nationally, I think they are the best. Our biggest rival was Michigan State University, which made for great hockey.

The night of the CCHA win was a special night. A win like that is hard to get. Our co-captains, Todd Flichel and Iain Duncan complimented each other on their leadership styles. They were definitely different. Todd was more laid back but he was very in tune with the players. He took players aside if needed. Iain was more vocal and direct.

I learned so much from Jerry York. He is the reason I got into coaching. He teaches you about life as much as hockey. He let players be themselves and allowed their talent to shine through. You learned the "why" behind the decisions he made. He wasn't always about x's and o's. It was also about how you conducted yourself and how you treat people. Jerry never liked cliques. He moved players around to spend time together so it wasn't all one-sided. He definitely taught lifelong lessons.

If we lost a game he would say, "It wasn't our night and here's what we have to do better next time." He always stayed positive and optimistic. Everyone needed to be on time for practice, meetings, game day and getting on the bus for away games. The only time that mattered was the time on

Jerry's watch. Some may have learned that lesson the hard way but then you never forget it.

My memories of Terry Flanagan were that he was a genuine and humble person. He always had the players' best interest at heart. He was a throwback to old-fashioned values.

Marc Potvin was a team player. He also had a big heart and would do anything for his teammates. He had everyone's back. He had inner drive and determination. He was a big and strong guy around the net and he would fight if he had to. He was well loved and a special guy. Marc believed in himself and did the work.

Greg Parks rose to challenges with determination and never backed down. He was a pistol. He felt he was the best and kept that mindset. I remember we were getting ready to play Michigan Sate and they had a guy on their team named, Joe Murphy. Greg went into Jerry's office and said, "I want to play against this guy because I am going to shut him down." Greg wanted to go up against Joe. He wanted that challenge. Greg was an edgy guy. I know he may have rubbed some of the guys the wrong way. He left nothing on the table. He was a competitor both on and off the ice. He would not take a backseat to anyone.

BG hockey will always have a special place in my heart.

My advice to players is to enjoy the whole experience. The people are what make Bowling Green.

Kevin Mann, Graduate Assistant

Kevin Mann, Graduate Assistant

I grew up in Western Canada. I loved watching the New York Islanders, Montreal Canadiens and the Toronto Maple Leafs. Hockey was in my blood ever since I was a kid.

I received a scholarship to play at the University of Maine for college hockey. I played there from 1983 to 1986. When I graduated from Maine, I was looking to get a graduate assistant position. My coach, Shawn Walsh, suggested that I reach out to a few colleges for a graduate assistant position. He encouraged me to contact Jerry York at Bowling Green State University. As luck would have it, Jerry was in need of a graduate assistant so I consider myself very fortunate to have gotten the position. I didn't know anyone at Bowling Green at the time. I just showed up with my belongings. Looking back, it really was a special time.

I always felt Bowling Green was an amazing place. It's a small town and it felt natural to be there because it reminded me of where I was from. I loved it from the minute I stepped on campus. I remember Jerry York picked me up from the airport. He helped me out a lot. I remember him always being surrounded by great people. (Buddy Powers, Terry Flanagan and Wayne Wilson). I learned so much from each of them. It was an incredible time.

I was actually planning to stay one more year at BG after I finished graduate school but an assistant coaching position opened up at the University of Illinois-Chicago. Their team was in the same league as Bowling Green. To be honest, I really did not want to leave BG but Jerry told me it was a good move for me so I accepted the position. At first, I was horrified to arrive in the big city of Chicago after being in Bowling Green. I missed the small town and now had to get used to a big city.

When the Falcons won the CCHA title in 1987, I truly felt like I was part of the team. I always thought the co-captains; Todd Flichel and Iain Duncan lead the team very well. Jerry York let them lead. I was so proud of them and the entire team. I saw how hard everyone worked at practice and how much they cared for each other. That culture was built long before I arrived.

So I soaked in everything I could like a sponge. That team had so many strengths and Jerry allowed each of them to do what they did best.

I think BG hockey fans are THE best. I remember the excitement from the fans. The players felt that excitement, too. It was an unbelievable run that year. Tickets were tough to get during that season. They were like golden tickets.

Jerry York was truly a mentor for me. He is a mentor among young men. He had integrity and class. He was always about building character. He communicated well. Everything he did was intentional. He is the winningest coach for a reason. He always had a plan.

I learned to become a better person from Jerry, Buddy, Terry and Wayne. It has stuck with me. The players can teach you just as much as the coaches can. I am so proud to have been a graduate assistant for that team.

For my memories about Terry Flanagan, we rode in the car a lot with Buddy to recruit. You learn a lot about people during long car rides. Terry was a caring person and a wonderful guy. His heart was as big as gold. He was someone you could joke around with. I loved him.

Marc Potvin was as tough as nails. His loss really got to me. It surprised me. I wish I had more time to know him better.

Greg Parks was a great teammate and a great locker room guy. He was full of energy and gave his all.

I would love to see BGSU hockey get back to its days of dominance. It happened before; it can happen again. I believe it can happen.

My advice for young hockey players is to not rush the process. Go where you are wanted. I hope players can learn what a special place BGSU is and what it means to play there.

The Players

Paul Connell #1 Goalie

Paul Connell #1, Goalie

I first became interested in playing hockey because my father, Bob Connell, was the high school hockey coach for our local school, Cranston West. Plus, my older brother, Tom, and twin brother, Peter, also played hockey so you can say hockey was in our blood.

The NHL players that I admired were Bobby Orr and Gerry Cheevers since growing up in New England. In the 70's, the Boston Bruins were king and they embodied the heart and soul to me for a winning team. I met Gerry Cheevers and I still have the photo today.

I was playing in the Rhode Island high school All-Star game and unbeknownst to me, Coach Buddy Powers was in attendance. I only played the third period but I, luckily, had a very good game. Coach Powers called me at my house the next day and told me that he watched me play and said I played well. He asked me what happened on the two goals that were scored on me and I gave him my assessment. He then asked me if I would be interested in going to Bowling Green. It was a no-brainer decision as they had just won the national title two years prior.

My reflections on my time at BG paint a picture of a deeply enriching and transformative experience. The sense of community, the incredible friendships (that last until today), the balance between academics and athletics, the personal growth, and the strong legacy of the hockey program all contributed to making my time at BG memorable and impactful. My pride and gratitude for my BG experience are evident in my detailed reflections, highlighting the importance of the supportive environment and the lasting bonds formed during my college years.

Winning the CCHA title: I was on the bench as a backup goalie, which allowed me to observe everything closely. The fans were packed into the stands, creating a sea of excitement and anticipation. The game itself was tough and closely contested, with emotions running high. As the final buzzer sounded, signaling our victory, an overwhelming sense of elation and sheer joy swept over us. The players and fans erupted in celebration, creating a scene of pure jubilation. I remember the fans piling on top of each other, capturing the moment in photographs, and the immense sense of achievement that filled the arena.

I have deep admiration and gratitude for the hockey fans. They truly had unwavering support and enthusiasm for the team. I want to share a memorable story that encapsulates the special relationship between the players and the fans. During my freshman year, I was grocery shopping in my hockey sweats when a young boy, about 10 years old, approached me and asked for my autograph. This moment was deeply touching for me. I was taken aback by the recognition and appreciation from such a young fan. The boy's excitement and gratitude left a lasting impression on me, making me realize the significant impact my teammates and I had on the community. This encounter exemplified the genuine admiration and support the fans had for us, regardless of our status on the team.

One thing that stood out to me about Coach York's guidance and leadership was his emphasis on discipline and consistency. He was very strict about certain rules, such as attending classes. This emphasis on discipline extended beyond the rink, reinforcing the importance of academics and personal responsibility. The strict discipline enforced by Coach York taught me the importance of responsibility and accountability. These values were not just applicable to hockey but were life lessons that I carried with me beyond my college years and today.

My freshman year felt like a period of sensory overload, where I had to navigate numerous new experiences simultaneously. The lessons learned about handling adversity, embracing team spirit, and upholding personal values and ethics had a lasting impact on my life. My time at BG was a transformative experience that shaped my identity and prepared me for future successes and challenges.

Remembering Terry Flanagan: I recall a personal story where Terry provided me with emotional support during a time when I felt out of place and was struggling with typical freshman year challenges. Terry reassured me by explaining that the ribbing and teasing I received from teammates were signs of acceptance and camaraderie. This conversation helped me feel more included and valued within the team, demonstrating Terry's ability to provide not just technical guidance but also emotional support to us players.

Marc Potvin: Marc was a confident, driven, and protective individual. He was my roommate and was the first person I met on campus since my recruiting visit occurred during the offseason. I had not met any of the players. We developed a tight bond and Marc was very protective of me, by intervening if anyone bothered me, showing his caring and protective side. On the ice, Marc was a fierce competitor who outworked everyone else. He had a reputation for being tough and fearless, qualities that made him a formidable player. I admired Marc's ability to balance confidence with hard work, considering him an inspirational figure. I miss him dearly.

Greg Parks: Greg was an incredibly skilled and intense player with a high hockey IQ. Greg was fearless on the ice, unafraid to take on larger opponents and perform under pressure. This fearless attitude earned him the respect of both fans and teammates. Off the ice, Greg had a confident and sometimes cocky demeanor, but he always backed it up, which I truly respected and admired. Greg was a crucial player whose contributions were vital to our team's success. He is truly missed.

My thoughts about BG hockey include deep pride, gratitude, and a sense of enduring connection. The program's rich legacy, the unwavering support from the community and fans, the resilience during challenging times, and the personal impact of the experience all contribute to my positive view of BG hockey. The program has significantly shaped my identity, and the lasting bonds formed during my time at BG continue to be an essential part of my life.

Advice: Mental preparation and resilience are crucial for new players joining the Bowling Green (BG) hockey program. Adversity is a natural part of the journey, and how you handle it can significantly impact your success and development.

I want to take this opportunity to express my deep gratitude for the unwavering support of my parents, Bob and Delores Connell. Their dedication and commitment were vital to my success and well-being during my time at Bowling Green. I would like to extend my gratitude for the relationships and bonds formed with my teammates, coaches, and equipment manager, Don Woods. These relationships were integral to my positive experience at BG.

Tom Pratt #2 Defenseman

Tom Pratt #2, Defenseman

I'm from Lake Placid, New York. My dad was a hockey player and a hockey coach. He was the hockey coach at my high school. So, hockey has been part of my life from an early age. I was put on skates as a young child and I loved it.

I used to watch "Hockey Night in Canada" on television and always enjoyed watching Guy Lafleur and Ken Dryden who both played for the Montreal Canadiens. I have to say though I have a real affinity for the New York Islanders.

I spent my freshman and sophomore years playing hockey at St. Lawrence University. I was looking for an opportunity to transfer schools. Once I visited Bowling Green, I loved it. Being from Lake Placid, I was actually present for the game when the 1984 team won the NCAA in my hometown. I was aware of Bowling Green and their reputation.

I was a transfer from St. Lawrence. My father was roommates and teammates at St. Lawrence with Colgate Hockey Coach, Terry Slater when they were in college. When my dad let Terry Slater know that I wanted to transfer, Terry recommended me to his former assistant who was Buddy Powers. There was also a relationship with Jerry York who recruited players from my dad's Lake Placid High School hockey team so there were definitely connections.

I always thought BG Hockey fans were amazing and awesome. I remember the arena was always packed. The fans always added to the experience.
I remember fans always standing outside waiting for the doors to open to the arena. Sometimes Todd Flichel and I would stop and get pizzas for the fans while they were waiting.

I look back on our 86-87 team and think what an amazingly talented team we had. We should have won the NCAA that season as well.

I thought Coach Jerry York had a great reputation for holding people accountable. I was on the receiving end of that a few times but it came from the right place. His job was not only to win hockey games but to develop men as well. He does so in such a way that you respect him.

Remembering Terry Flanagan: Terry wore it on his sleeve. By that, I mean his emotions and his passion. He was fiery and fun. Whatever he was feeling, we knew it.

Marc Potvin: Marc was my "road roommate" when I was a senior and he was a freshman. Marc was such a nice guy. I enjoyed having him as a teammate.

Greg Parks: Greg was street savvy. He wasn't a big guy nor the fastest but he always shocked me with how good of a player he was. He was smart, slick and quick-witted.

My advice to any new hockey players is to enjoy what you are doing because it goes fast.

Todd Flichel #3 Defenseman
Co-Captain

Todd Flichel #3, Defenseman Co-Captain

Hockey was part of growing up in Canada. I liked watching hockey on TV when I was young and it just kind of progressed from there. I was always a hockey fan. Seeing these guys from the NHL was larger than life. Some of my favorite players were Darryl Sittler, Lanny McDonald, and Borje Salming who all played for the Toronto Maple Leafs.

I was playing for a junior team outside Ottawa (Canada). I really didn't know anything about college hockey in the United States. I remember coming home from school one day and my mom told me that Ralph Backstrom had called from Denver. He used to play for the Montreal Canadiens. Anyway, he wanted to know if I was interested in coming to the states to play. That was really the first time I ever thought about it. Those plans fell through but the following year, Buddy Powers and Terry Flanagan came to watch me play and I ended up going on my first recruiting visit to Bowling Green. It was opening weekend of the '82-'83 season and BG was playing Wisconsin. Jerry York made a scholarship offer for me to play at Bowling Green. I thought it happened pretty quickly. My parents were big supporters of me getting an education.

During that time, I was drafted by the Sudbury Wolves in the Ontario Hockey League. I was somewhat interested in that so I visited to check things out. But, I ended up going to Bowling Green. I was a small-town Canadian boy and Bowling Green had that same small town feel for me. It seemed to be a good fit with what I was comfortable with.

When I first came to Bowling Green for a hockey game, it was overwhelming at first. I had never seen anything like it. It was a very highly rated program. Section A, where the student fans sat, was going crazy. The hockey aspect of it was great.

When I was growing up, I was playing center but when I was a teenager one of my coaches had me switch to defense. Defense is about hard work. Offense is about creativity. I was more about logic and hard work. I was very good in Math class but not so much in English class. Another thing that worked in my favor was of course, my height. I was bigger than anyone else was and it made a good fit for playing defense.

When you have good experiences, which also includes winning games it helps to strengthen friendships. I still talk to Tom Pratt, George Roll and Eddie Powers. Good experiences cement friendships. There were many good comraderies. You can't win unless you are getting along with each other. We spent a lot of time together, which is important for team dynamic. There has to be friendship because you need it to make things work on the ice. You can't just turn it on and turn it off. It doesn't work that way.

When we got that CCHA win, it was such a relief. You let the emotions flow. We had a disappointing season the year before. But, we came back the following year and it was an awesome experience. Whenever I see the picture of Iain Duncan and me carrying the banner around and see myself screaming towards the sky, I am reminded of what a release of emotion that was.

Bowling Green fans seem to know the game and understand it so that is a big thing, too. I remember seeing all of the fans waiting outside whenever we arrived at the rink. When you have that kind of support and backing, it is a motivator and an energy lifter.

Jerry York was obviously a very talented coach. He definitely knew how to work with a bunch of different personalities and motivate us. You understand in hindsight the decisions he made and why, even if you didn't agree with it at the time. We were a pretty damn good team that year.

I learned to grow up at Bowling Green. There is much of what I do now that is still influenced by my experiences at BG. It has served me well. You gain confidence in yourself knowing that you can rise to challenges. You get some notoriety, which helps your confidence to move forward in life. On the flip side of that, you have to learn not to take it too far. There has to be a balance so you can learn from it.

I played for seven years after Bowling Green. I went from being a captain of a great team to being one in the crowd of 70 in a training camp. You are starting all over once more.

Remembering Terry Flanagan: He was really a good guy. I think as an assistant coach, his role was a little different in that he could be more like one of the guys. I had a lot of respect for him.

Marc Potvin: He was a freshman that year. I used to come back to BG over the summer when I was still playing. I have to say I probably got to know him better after Bowling Green than when I was at Bowling Green. If he was around during the summer, we would hang out together whether it was working out, skating or just having fun. I liked him a lot. He was a good guy.

Greg Parks: He was a pistol! He was someone you wanted on your team and definitely not someone you wanted to play against. He was an agitator type of guy but also a great guy. He was a hard worker. I really didn't have much of a connection with him after Bowling Green.

Advice: You have to believe in yourself. There will be a lot of challenges that you are going to face. You have to believe in yourself and rise to those challenges, not only in hockey but also in life. I have played with so many guys over the years who were talented but only about themselves. Be a good teammate. It is important to work together.

Scott Paluch #4 Defenseman

Scott Paluch #4, Defenseman

My start in hockey is a little bizarre. I grew up in Chicago and at that time, hockey wasn't as mainstream as it is now. I grew up in an athletic family but in the early days, I wasn't playing hockey. That was until one day I went to the barbershop and the regular barber wasn't there. The substitute barber happened to be the president of the local ice hockey association and he suggested I stop out and play hockey. So, my older brother and I did stop by to skate. My brother did not like it but I on the other hand loved it and wanted to play. I fell in love with hockey at seven years old. It was a non-traditional path. I loved the quickness of the game and the team aspect.

I always admired Denis Potvin of the New York Islanders.

Terry Flanagan and Buddy Powers recruited me to play for Bowling Green. I loved the support that the hockey team had. They were ranked number one at the time with the NCAA in '84 so, it was a no brainer that I was going to play at Bowling Green. I loved the atmosphere and how excited everyone seemed to be over hockey.

We had so many gifted defensemen that it never mattered who I was paired with on the ice because it was always great. We had each other's backs. We were certainly a talented team during that time. I feel we could have won the NCAA that season as well.

Our center guys were Paul Ysebaert, Greg Parks and Nelson Emerson. All three of them were amazing and all of them went on to the NHL. Back then, it was more difficult for college guys to play in the NHL but they all did.

One of the main pieces of BG Hockey is the fans. They care and were a big part of the reason that I wanted to play at BG. There was great synergy between student fans and community fans.

I was fortunate to view Jerry York's work from several different lenses. I played for him at Bowling Green and then worked with him at Bowling Green and at Boston College. What always struck me was his consistency with the way he works with people. It was always an unrelenting positive approach on a daily basis. He always had a bounce in his step regardless of the situation. He created a culture of doing the right thing both on and off the ice. You knew you were part of something special. We had so many great players. We were allowed to play the way we needed to, to be successful. Jerry treated everyone with respect and it was contagious. We had three coaches who were the best of the best: Jerry York, Buddy Powers and Terry Flanagan.

Remembering Terry Flanagan: He was a regular guy's guy. You wanted to be around hm. He was a great person and a great family man. He was one of the first coaches to contact me to play at Bowling Green. Both Terry and Buddy were the best compliments to Jerry.

Marc Potvin: He was a great teammate. He was the one who provided the laughter, if needed. He was definitely a physical force on the ice. He always had our backs.

Greg Parks: He was one of the most competitive players that I have ever been around. Everything was a challenge and a competition. That is how he approached the game and life. He was clearly the guy we needed and was a huge part of the team's success. He was always going to find a way to get the job done.

I still feel Bowling Green is one of the premier places to play college hockey. The program has certainly has had its ups and downs. We all want to see the continued success that was prevalent during the 70s, 80s and 90s. There is a unique connection between the student fans, community fans and the players. When a player comes to Bowling Green, they have the ability to play for the highest achievements in hockey. Plus, you have a community who cares about that success as well.

Advice to new hockey players: Embrace the opportunity to play for a great program and give it your all. Your individual goals and dreams are a big part of your journey. But, do no not lose sight of working with your coaches and teammates. It is a driving force that will influence the rest of your life.

Kevin Dahl #5 Defenseman

Kevin Dahl #5, Defenseman

Being a Canadian, there isn't much else to do in those cold winters so; hockey was just a sport we were raised with. It was a natural fit and went with our surroundings.

I remember seeing the success of other hockey players when I was growing up and always thought that maybe I could do that as well. Also, there is a social part of hockey, the friendships you make and the fun.

I always admired some of the players from the Toronto Maple Leafs such as Darryl Sittler, Borje Salming and Tiger Williams.

I played hockey in Stratford where several other Falcons had played before. Terry Flanagan was at Bowling Green as an assistant coach at that time so there was a good pipeline from Stratford to Bowling Green. Other players that came from Stratford were Chad Arthur, Nelson Emerson and Marc Potvin.

At the time I was recruited, Bowling Green hockey was number one, which was obviously impressive. I loved the arena, too. The fan support was great and so was the noise level.

I think I grew into my role as a defenseman. I was very young at the time. I was surrounded by a great group of established defensemen and I learned a lot from them. Every hockey team needs a strong, defensive core and we had that.

For the actual CCHA title win, I did not play that night due to an injury but I was there. I know it was a great experience for the guys who had been at Bowling Green for a while. They deserved it. But, it also taught the younger players, including myself, how to win. It was an incredible experience.

The fans are incredible at BG. I remember seeing long lines forming outside the arena before the games. The fans played a part in our winning. The fans were as loud as they could be. It was a great experience.

I was a seventeen-year-old freshman when I arrived at Bowling Green and had a lot to learn. I spent a lot of time working with Coach Buddy Powers on defense.

Coach Jerry York was very mindful of how things needed to be and what he expected of us. The combination of Jerry, Buddy and Terry was a great coaching team. Jerry would sometimes get upset with us but I don't think he really wanted to be upset. He wanted us to be a good team and to be good people.

I had to work to earn my spot on the ice because we had such a great team. Playing defense is hard position. I was working hard and striving to be in the lineup. There were so many great players that you had to earn your spot.

I remember Terry Flanigan as being a great person.

It is hard for me to talk about Marc Potvin. We've been friends since we were 16 years old and that's all I can say at this time.

I will always remember Greg Parks as being a fierce competitor. He was a great player.

Advice: Besides the love of the game itself, you're going to meet some lifelong friends.

Thad Rusiecki #6 Defenseman

Thad Rusiecki #6, Defenseman

I grew up in Massachusetts. My older brothers played hockey. I started skating when I was four years old. I always admired Larry Robinson who played for the Montreal Canadiens. I thought he was a defensive defenseman who played the game with toughness and determination.

One of my biggest influences that made me want to continue to play hockey was when I was 15 years old. I was chosen to play for a Junior A-team in Western New England. Gary Dineen was very well known. He briefly played in the NHL and played on the Canadian Olympic Hockey Team. He was an incredible motivator and you wanted to play for him. He was instrumental in helping players get into college. He felt that getting an education as well as playing hockey were very important. Gary provided many opportunities. I remember participating in Hockey Night in Boston, which is where Coach Buddy Powers saw me play. Shortly thereafter, he contacted me about playing hockey for Bowling Green. I have very vivid memories of Buddy picking me up at the airport in Detroit.

I thought the people in Bowling Green were kind and genuine. Playing at the ice arena was an incredible experience. I played on the penalty-killing unit that went against the opponent's power play. It was also something I enjoyed. Each and every game was sold out. The noise of the fans was absolutely incredible. We were lucky. It was a magnificent arena to play hockey.

I remember sitting in the locker room and hearing the fans outside banging on the doors. I would get chills just listening to them. It was exciting to know that they were there to support us. Once the fans came in and were seated then you could hear everyone chanting, B-G-S-U! It was an experience that I will never forget. BG has the best fans. I was awestruck at the support we had.

When the final buzzer went off on the night we won the CCHA, I remember looking over at Kruzer (Gary Kruzich, goalie) and he threw his gear into the air. It was an explosion. The glass in the arena was low at the time so we were able to interact with fans as we skated around. It was a great moment to be part of something special.

I remember hearing the song, "We Built this City" (Jefferson Starship) playing inside the locker room on the radio. Every time I hear that song, I am reminded of those days waiting in the locker room to take the ice and what a great feeling it was.

I was fortunate to play with some outstanding players. We had great success during that time. Buddy Powers pushed me to do better. Jerry York was a very disciplined coach. He provided structure, which is what we needed. He was always positive. I remember him saying, "It's a great day to be a Falcon, right Thad?" He cared about people. It wasn't just about the wins.

Remembering Terry Flanagan: I remember Terry was always smiling. He was positive and honest. He was great to laugh with and share a joke with. He was very smart with technique.

Marc Potvin: Marc was an extreme competitor. He was the protector. He had a tough exterior but a very big heart.

Greg Parks: Greg was the guy who never wanted to lose. He wasn't the biggest guy but his skill level was incredible. He was part of our success.

Advice: Bowling Green Hockey has an unbelievable tradition. Stick with that tradition. You need to uphold what all of the other players have done before you. It means something when you become a Falcon.

Brian McKee #7 Defenseman

Brian McKee #7, Defenseman

I was born in Toronto so becoming interested in hockey was second nature. As soon as my twin brother Brad and I learned to walk, we were on skates. We joined a league when we were five years old. My oldest brother Ken taught Brad and I all of our fundamental skills.

I loved playing hockey. I loved the game and the competition. It was complete passion. I always challenged myself at every game. I would have to say I enjoyed watching all of the players for the Toronto Maple Leafs. I always admired their ability to show up and perform.

I went on recruitment trips to Ferris State (Michigan) and to Bowling Green. I loved Bowling Green. Terry Flanagan recruited me and Buddy Powers came to see me play.

I love Bowling Green to this day. Being there was one of the best things that has ever happened in my life. I felt Jerry York was a phenomenal leader. Jerry York is a brilliant coach and motivator. I have so much respect for him.

I felt I had talent and definitely could play but if I needed a kick in the butt, I got that, too! I learned a lot. I was known for my slap shot. I wasn't the biggest. I wasn't the strongest but I could read plays. I loved the power plays.

I will admit that I was mouthy and it often got me into trouble. I remember when we were playing in a tournament in New York and Coach York warned me to "button it up". I didn't listen, so what happened next? I received a 10-minute misconduct for mouthing off to the referee. Looking back, I got what I deserved. It definitely was a big lesson. I was taught so much in the years I was at Bowling Green. Buddy Powers was a great influence on my career.

BG Hockey fans are absolutely awesome. They are unbelievable. It was always flattering to see the fans waiting outside on game night. It made you want to do your best to make everyone happy. It was an exciting time.

I wear my CCHA Championship ring all the time. If I don't have it on then I feel like I am missing something.

Remembering Terry Flanagan: I think he was more of a scouting coach. He seemed to be on the road a lot. He had such a positive attitude. He was a super nice guy. There was never a negative vibe with Terry.

Marc Potvin: I only played with Marc for one year. I thought he was a good kid. He was a big guy – solid. He was a force.

Greg Parks: We respected each other but our personalities didn't click that well. We did butt heads to be honest. But, he was a great player.

Advice: Don't ever think that you are bigger than the game. Always be willing to learn and work your butt off. Bowling Green has a great hockey program. I am proud of what we accomplished.

Alan Leggett #8 Defenseman

Alan Leggett #8, Defenseman

I grew up in a very small town in rural Alberta, Canada. The population was about 4,000 people. I had the skates on by or before age five. Hockey was what we lived and breathed. My dad, brothers and sister all played hockey. It was part of our life. I was a huge Montreal Canadiens fan even when I lived in the land of Wayne Gretzky and the Edmonton Oilers.

I was playing for a team called the Hobbema Hawks. One day my coach asked me if I was interested in playing hockey at the college level. Until that point in time, I hadn't thought about playing college hockey in the United States. I wasn't aware that there was college hockey in the United States. He said there was someone that was going to attend the game, watch me play and wanted to talk with me afterward. That person turned out to be Buddy Powers. He invited me to visit Bowling Green and that was how it all started.

Visiting Bowling Green was the first time I had been in the United States. It was a bit of wonder. The hockey program was quite impressive.

I spent a lot of time keeping up with my studies, which has served me well. I made many good friendships. Even though we haven't seen each other in years, I feel we are close enough that if we saw each other now, we would pick up where we left off.

When we won the CCHA title, it was because we were at the top. Michigan State was also up for that title and they were always our biggest rival. It was great to win.

Bowling Green fans definitely spoil you. You expect to see fans like that everywhere you go. Of course, I am biased. They made playing for Bowling Green an amazing time.

It is difficult to pin down into proper words what it was like to play for Coach Jerry York. I definitely grew as a better player and person because of him. He had strong integrity. He was fair and honest with everyone.

Remembering Terry Flanagan: Terry always had a smile on his face. He was a positive force for us. He was a great influence.

Marc Potvin: Marc was fun and always seemed to be laughing. I thought he had positive energy. He made a great teammate.

Greg Parks: Greg and I were roommates. He was definitely intense on the ice and that's what you want. Off the ice, I thought he was a fun-loving guy, a good friend and teammate.

I am very proud to have been part of the hockey program at BG. The talent we had was incredible so being there was a phenomenal experience. The coaches, teammates, fans and the community were tied together. It was a privilege to be asked to play for BG.

Advice: Believe in yourself. I know sometimes it can be hard but you need to put in the work and stay dedicated. Find the balance between on the ice and off the ice.

Rob Urban #10 Forward

Rob Urban #10, Forward

In what seems to be only five or six strides after stepping out onto the ice, I am already crossing the red line. A cool breeze blows on my face and through my helmetless head of hair. Resonating in my mind are the words: "Wild, Crazy, Poised"*. Fans from our "sold-out" arena continue to roar their ear-piercing cheers. This notches up the high energy level already established by BGSU pep band as it finishes the first stanza of the theme from the movie Rocky, now affectionately known to us as Rocky Hockey. If we could, we would give every screaming BG fan who was leaning over the protective glass a high five. This is how every home game began for our 1986-87 team.

In 1967, when my parents and I moved to Minnetonka, Minnesota from Philadelphia, hockey was new to us; my brother Jeff was born soon after our arrival. But, we had a large pond no more than 100 yards from our new home, and a neighborhood full of young families whose boys made sure that the ice was always clear. Family skating was on one side and intense hockey competition on the other. Every winter, essentially from Thanksgiving to Easter, hockey became a dominant part of my life, and that of Jeff who would later play for the University of Michigan.

As a three year old, I began skating on the family side of that pond, first learning how to stand on skates, then how to run on skates, and then how to push and glide (though many still claim I never got past the running part). Jeff soon followed. As soon as it appeared that we could keep pace, we were invited to join the hockey games. Even after we started to play organized hockey on municipal teams, we always returned to that pond. With only three channels on TV, if a young boy was going to do something in his free time during the cold Minnesota winters, it was probably going to be pond hockey.

My first favorite NHL player was Bill Goldsworthy of the Minnesota North Stars. Whenever he scored a goal, he celebrated with his "Goldy Shuffle fist pump". So, that is what we would do too as little kids. Like perhaps all of us on my '86-87 BG team, I wanted to be an NHL hockey player. But, was that possible? Follow your dreams we are told. In Bantams and in high school I excelled on teams that made strong runs for the Minnesota State championship. However, I was also a somewhat awkward skater. But, why not give it a shot? At that time, the road to the NHL for American players was almost always through a Division 1 college program. That was my first objective.

High school hockey was both frustrating and rewarding for me. I was a high performance player, but I was plagued with injuries each year that significantly reduced my playing time. Nevertheless, I was present for the "big games", and led our teams in scoring during my final two years when we exceeded expectations and lifted our school program to the top level in Minnesota high school hockey. College scouts contacted me, but I was crushed when on multiple occasions they came to see me play but I was injured and in the stands.

At the end of my senior year season, I received a call from Jerry York who invited me to visit Bowling Green. My father and I were able to attend the end of season hockey banquet, and that visit opened our eyes to an extremely well run college hockey program that was in its prime. At that banquet, there was a strong sense that the following season (what would be our 1984 NCAA championship season) would be a very special one, and I knew I wanted to be a part of it. So when Coach York offered a scholarship, I immediately accepted.

Given the level of talent on that 1983-84 team, it may have been a mistake to write off so early my aspirations to play in the NHL, but I was determined to not let that "awakening" negatively affect me. Instead, I changed my focus to lifting weights, becoming stronger and molding myself into the best player I could be so as to compliment, and add value to, the many super talented players that were on my four different Bowling Green teams.

The BGSU campus has a large and successful Fraternity system, but our BG hockey team was very much its own fraternity, or band of brothers, both on and off the ice. The camaraderie and support was exceptional, and it was my teammates with whom I spent most of my time. During my freshman year, I shared a dorm room with Gary Kruzich, and although he is no longer a part of my life, he like so many of my other teammates, remains in my heart.

After our freshman year, all my teammates in my class moved out of the campus dorms, but we moved-in with non-teammate housemates. This was healthy, and provided balance and a break from the pressures of hockey. We would still be together most every day and a majority of the evenings, whether relaxing at Mark's Pub, the Brathaus, the Uptown Bar, or Saturday night after-hour parties when we needed a little extra time to unwind after high pressure Friday and Saturday night games. Many of those Saturday after-hour parties were hosted at my place at 808 Wooster with my very tolerant and supportive housemates, Steve, Ed, Blaise, Jim, Dave and Tess.

A very special part of my experience at Bowling Green was the host family program. Tom and Jean Bamburowski, and their two children Brent and David, made Bowling Green a home for me during those four years. Their warmth and hospitality shown to me was priceless. When I look back at my time at Bowling Green, they are an indelible part of those years and I still love them.

I also must acknowledge head coach Jerry York, and coaches Buddy Powers and Terry Flanagan, who accompanied me during all four of my years at Bowling Green. Each played a different role as both coach and teacher. It is not difficult to see why Jerry, with his vision, philosophy and style, went on to become the most successful coach in NCAA hockey history.

This book focuses on our 1986-87 Bowing Green ice hockey team, my senior year. We were ranked number 1 or 2 for most of that season and made a legitimate run for a second NCAA Championship. We won the CCHA league title, but then lost in the finals of the CCHA playoffs in double-overtime. This loss forced us to go on the road for the first round of the NCAA Tournament Final Eight. There, we were eliminated in a relative upset by a very good Harvard team. Had we played at home, in front of our own fans, the result could very well have been different.

From a player's point of view, although we fell short, I look back at a very talented team that carved out a very successful season, in front of a fantastic and always energetic home fan base. From a personal point of view this was enhanced by an incredibly rich life experience at Bowling Green, one shared with quality teammates, dear friends, very special BGSU hockey fans, and so many others who unfortunately there was just not enough time to get to know better.

"Wild, Crazy, Poised" - these are words that prior to every game (both home and away) were posted above the locker room exit door, that leads to the ice surface, by our veteran equipment manager Don "Woody" Woods.

Paul Ysebaert #11 Center

Paul Ysebaert #11, Center

We lived near a construction company when I was growing up. The building had a water run-off that would eventually turn into a pretty good-sized pond and freeze in the winter. That's where my sisters taught me how to skate. I remember my dad putting tires down on the ice to create hockey drills. I would skate around those tires all day. We also worked on passing pucks. I loved the whole experience.

When I was about seven years old, I started playing in what was called a "house league" for hockey on Saturday mornings. I liked playing baseball, too. At age 13 is when I really decided that I wanted to play hockey and stick with it.

My cousin, Mike Crombeen played in the NHL (Cleveland Barons, St. Louis Blues and Hartford Whalers). I remember staying at his house for a while when I was young. Mike was definitely a positive influence in my life.

Wayne Gretzky was my idol. I had a poster on the ceiling of Wayne Gretzky above my bed. The poster would be the first thing I would see in the morning and the last thing I would see at night. It was all visual imagery to work towards what I wanted to do with my life. I used to watch and read everything I could about him. The first time I met Wayne is when I tried out for Team Canada. We had played two games in New Foundland and I found myself next to him on the bench. If he undid his skates, then I would undo mine. I also taped my hockey stick the way he taped his. I taped my shinpads the way he taped his. I was doing my best to mimic him. And I actually kept those same rituals during my whole hockey career.

I didn't even know about college hockey. One day, I remember my dad telling me that someone from Bowling Green had called. Jerry York, Buddy Powers and Terry Flanagan had actually been to a game to see me play the night before in Sarnia (Canada). So, the next day my dad and I had breakfast with Jerry, Buddy and Terry. The coaches offered me a full ride to Bowling Green. I liked the campus. It was close to home. It didn't feel overwhelming.

I was recruited by several other schools but I chose Bowling Green. The team had won the NCAA the previous year. They were all professionals.

I had never seen crowds like the BG hockey fans. They made BG hockey. I fed off of that. Winning the CCHA was icing on the cake. We had a great team that year.

Jerry York was a demanding coach because he wanted the best from you. He never wavered. He was solid and made us well prepared for every single game. I learned a lot during practice, too. Bowling Green hockey had great leaders.

Remembering Terry Flanagan: Terry was a genuine person and coach. He and Buddy Powers were the perfect assistants for Jerry and for us. Terry knew how to push the right buttons during the week-long practices leading up to weekend games. The whole Flanagan family was all about hockey and he passed his motivation onto us.

Marc Potvin: He wasn't afraid. He learned his role and didn't go beyond his abilities which helped us rely on him.

Greg Parks: He was feisty. He played bigger than he was and had a great work ethic. He reminded me of a pest you didn't want to play against shift after shift.

All three of them left this earth way too soon.

Advice: You're given every opportunity to be the best you can be. Take advantage of everything because it sets you up for whatever else will follow. You need to work just as hard on your academics as you do on the ice. It's important to get your degree. You need to work harder than you think because there is always someone else working harder than you. If you enjoy the game, play as long as you can.

Mark Lori #12 Right Wing

Mark Lori #12, Right Wing

I grew up in Canada and playing hockey is pretty much how you pass the time during the winter. Skating on frozen ponds was a past time, too. I'm one of eight kids so I played a lot with my older brothers and my twin brother.

I always felt I was good at playing hockey. I enjoyed it. I liked the competition and the camaraderie in the locker room so I stuck with it.

I admired Bobby Orr (Boston Bruins) and Phil Esposito (Chicago Blackhawks, Boston Bruins and New York Rangers). Hockey is a tough sport played by tough guys.

At first, I had a scholarship to play at Northeastern University in Boston. I played there for two years. But, after my second year, I wanted to transfer and play closer to home. At that time, I had a younger brother who was undergoing cancer treatment for leukemia in Toronto.

I had known Mike Natyshak for a long time and of course, he was at Bowling Green when I was at Northeastern. I had talked to him and then one thing led to another. That's how I met Jerry York and Buddy Powers. Through them, I was able to transfer to Bowling Green and start my junior year.

Bowling Green was a complete change from Northeastern in Boston. Bowling Green was more country, rural and small but I loved it. The hockey team was a big deal and I fell in love with the whole environment.

When you are part of a team that has anywhere between 26 to 28 guys, you are going to become tight with some of them and form strong friendships. It was fun. We were all working together to win.

I thought Coach Jerry York was a very good teacher of the game and ran things efficiently at practice.

Remembering Terry Flanigan: He was a great guy. He was energetic. He cared about us, the game and winning. He was a guy you wanted to play hard for.

Marc Potvin: Marc was a good guy. He was there if you needed him. A big body and a big personality. I enjoyed my time knowing him.

Greg Parks: Greg and I lived together for one year. He was feisty and ornery but not in a bad way. He was someone you wanted on your team. He was hard to play against. We had some great laughs together and some good times. When he passed away, I was heartbroken.

I'm glad BG hockey is still on its feet and doing well. I have a lot of fond memories. The level of talent on the 86-87 team was tremendous. We were definitely tight.

Advice: The skills, work ethic and discipline you learn will carry over into other aspects of your life. You do what is best for the team and contribute your part. You do what is asked of you. Hockey is a sport you need to play with positive energy and a lot of enthusiasm.

Andy Gribble #13 Right Wing

Andy Gribble #13, Right Wing

I grew up in Toronto, which is the center of the universe for hockey. I started skating around age three. When I was older, I played one year as a goalie and that didn't work. I liked moving in front of the net instead.

When you play on a team, you establish comradery. This carries over into any career in life. When you work with others, you can tell who is a team player.

At age 16, I was diagnosed with being a Type 1 diabetic. I lost 30 pounds. Once I was on proper meds, my hockey improved because I was in better shape. I tried to keep that information on the down low. I realize now that I could have helped someone else at the time who may have had the same diagnosis. I had kept quiet about it as much as possible because I did not want anything to change about how people perceived my playing or me.

I had offers to attend Brown University, Ferris State, Michigan, Western Michigan and Miami. I chose Bowling Green because they had won the national championship. Terry Flanagan and Buddy Powers had recruited me to play at Bowling Green.

Brian Meharry and I played Junior B hockey together. He was being recruited by Bowling Green as well. So, we both went! How could you go wrong by attending a school where the hockey team had won the NCAA?

We were a great team. We were there to support each other. I wish I had kept in better touch with my teammates after BG.

Bowling Green hockey fans are the best! The fans are outstanding. There was always great support. You gave it your all and you played to win. If the fan support wasn't as strong as it was, I don't think we would have had the success we had.

Regarding the hockey movie Youngblood (1986) starring Rob Lowe, Patrick Swayze and Keanu Reeves: It was late August or early September of 1984. Brian Meharry and I were practicing at a rink in Toronto with some other players when a guy showed up at the rink and asked if we wanted to be extras in a move. I think about eight of us agreed. They started filming a month or so later. Brian played on the team that was Rob Lowe's team and the focus of the movie. Their team was called the Hamilton Mustangs. I, on the other hand, played on the rougher team, their opponent, and that team was called the Thunder Bay Bombers. It was definitely a fun and memorable experience.

I think Coach Jerry York is the grand poohbah of hockey coaches. He was such a successful coach and a wonderful guy. He needed to keep us at arm's length because of his role. It was more of the assistant coaches with who we had closer rapport. Each coach had a different role and a different approach.

Remembering Terry Flanagan: He was a funny guy and a really down to earth person.

Marc Potvin: He was a character. I thought he was a fun and quality guy. He was a big, solid, physical player. He would stand up for you.

Greg Parks: He was a terrific hockey player. He wasn't a big guy but he was fast. He always got the job done. He was an agitator but it worked for him.

Advice: You will learn to grow up at Bowling Green. We were definitely spoiled. We got a lot of attention but then the real world hits you and then you realize you're on your own. It's important to work hard. Network and build connections. Be willing to accept constructive criticism. Give it your best effort.

Marc Potvin #14 Right Wing

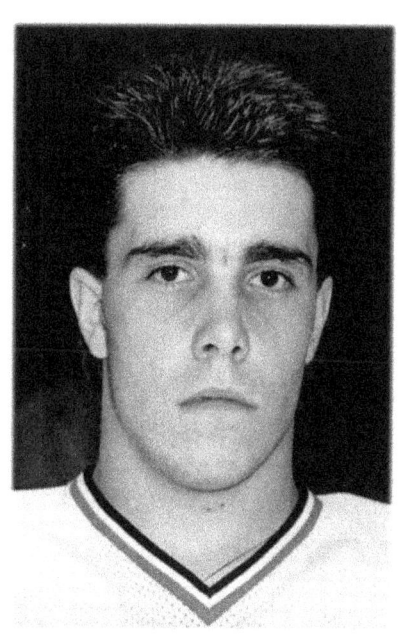

In memory of Marc Potvin #14, Right Wing
Interview provided by Marc's widow, Maria Potvin

I came to Bowling Green on a full ride scholarship for Gymnastics. I loved the campus and the Gymnastics Program. It also wasn't too far from my hometown of North Canton, Ohio. My major was a BA in Communications with a specialization in Marketing.

Marc and I met by chance one evening at Mark's Pizza Pub! Our gymnastics team had won the MAC championship and for Marc, it was the CCHA Championship for hockey. So, we both had just won championships in our respective sports and the fact that we were both athletes were definitely an automatic match. I was instantly drawn to him with his crazy personality and fun spirit! We always had so much fun together. We became great friends first before we started dating and then we ended up being soulmates.

I have to be honest; I was never a hockey fan until I attended Bowling Green. I'll never forget the first game I attended. All of the fans were holding up the newspapers and when the opposing team was announced we would hold up the newspapers as though we were reading them and then shout, "WHO'S HE? NOBODY!" The BGSU hockey fans were the absolute best. Opposing teams hated playing in our barn.

Marc was always larger than life! He was the first to any party and the last one to leave. In fact, he was the life of the party. This crazy zest for life carried over into the locker room and his role on the hockey team. He loved hockey and all that it empowered him to be. He grew up in Canada and started skating at the age of two. His dream was to make it to the NHL one day and BGSU was his pathway to get there. He loved playing hockey and being around the guys. Two of his lifelong friends were the best men in our wedding, Kevin Dahl and Bruce Kratt. I have so many fond memories from our days together at BGSU and I wouldn't trade them for the world.

Greg Parks #15 Center

In Memory of Greg Parks #15, Center
Greg's mother, Bonnie Parks, has contributed her thoughts in his memory.

Greg became interested in hockey at a very young age. He started skating at age four or five and soon was part of the community hockey program in Edmonton, Alberta (Canada). Through the years, Greg and his brother Malcolm spent many hours shooting pucks in our basement and at the local rink. It was always Greg's dream to have a career in hockey and decided to attend a university. Malcolm also chose a university and played for the University of North Dakota from 1983 to 1987.

Without a doubt, Wayne Gretzky was Greg's favorite NHL player. Greg had a great sense of humor and as a young fellow; he got a kick out of signing notes to family and friends as, "Gretz".

Greg was recruited at age 16 while in eleventh grade. At the time, he was playing for the St. Albert Saints in the AJHL. As a recruit, Greg had the opportunity to visit Bowling Green and a few other universities. He chose Bowling Green without hesitation. He knew they had a great hockey program and a well-recognized business school. He felt welcomed and comfortable.

There are fond memories of Buddy Powers and Terry Flanagan recruiting Greg and visiting our home.

I always thought the Bowling Green hockey fans were very enthusiastic and devoted which made for a fun atmosphere during games.

I remember an active community that went the extra mile to make sure visiting families felt welcomed. On occasion, there were Bowling Green families that hosted Sunday dinners to the players. A home cooked meal was always something they looked forward to and appreciated.

The hockey program at Bowling Green brought players, students and fans from near and far which added strength. BG has a very successful and recognized hockey program, which makes it a destination for many new players.

During his time at Bowling Green, Greg had several good friends from the team. He considered his roommates and his teammates to be his friends. He made many lasting and treasured friendships. The "Falcons" were definitely a strong and loyal unit. Our family is forever grateful to Joe Quinn for orchestrating "Parksy Stories from Bowling Green".

After meeting Coach Jerry York, my husband and I felt very comfortable that he would be coaching our son. I have fond memories of enjoying a wonderful dinner and evening in the York's home. They were so hospitable. I feel confident in saying that Greg had a great deal of respect for Jerry York, his professionalism, his decision-making and the fact that he was very approachable. Greg always wanted to give 100% for Jerry and the team.

Greg was very loyal and proud to be a Falcon. He was passionate about the game. He enjoyed four wonderful years at BGSU. Those years were part of the foundation that led to the next 14 years of his successful hockey career, playing mostly in Europe. Winning the Calder Cup in 1989 and the Olympic Silver Medal for Canada in 1994 were definite highlights for Greg.

Don Barber #16, Left Wing

Every effort was made to locate and contact Don Barber to participate in this book project. Unfortunately, we were not successful in our attempts but have fond memories of his time on the ice at BGSU.

Geoff Williams #17, Forward

Several efforts to locate Geoff Williams have been exhausted. Unfortunately, we were unable to locate him for this book project.

Brent Regan #18 Defenseman

Brent Regan #18, Defenseman

Being a youngster from western Canada, I think everyone learns to skate about the same time they learn to walk. It is just part of the culture. I started being interested in hockey at age five. I loved watching Hockey Night in Canada. It was always a dream of mine to play hockey. I considered hockey my life and how I defined myself. Its how you look at yourself, how others look at you and of course how the girls see you. It all goes together. You're getting adoration. You get to a point where you believe it's going to continue and then you get a false sense of security that you're invincible.

I always admired Bobby Orr and Guy Lafleur in the NHL. They were fast. They were the best.

I was playing for the St. Albert Saints. There was heavy scouting happening in western Canada. I was scouted by several different schools such as Ohio State, Michigan State and even Harvard. Then I went on a recruiting trip to Bowling Green. BG was ranked number one in the country at the time. It was the place you wanted to be if you were a hockey player. Terry Flanagan recruited me.

I always thought our team got along overall as a group. Naturally, there were smaller groups of friends within the team but overall, I felt we were a pretty tight community.

Bowling Green hockey fans took things seriously. Playing in front of home crowds made it special. There were awesome. It seemed like everyone knew our names. You were kind of like a celebrity. The environment definitely places you on a pedestal.

Coach Jerry York sometimes drove me crazy and to be honest, I needed to be driven crazy. I had a bit of an attitude. He would call me into his office and told me to step it up if I needed it. He was a brilliant coach and a brilliant human. He always moved with good intention. He was selfless, cared about the team and did what was best for us. He treated us as we needed to be treated and that made us work on the ice. The coaching relationship between he and Buddy Powers was the perfect dynamic.

Remembering Terry Flanagan: He was so kind. He had a great outlook on life and was always positive and smiling.

Marc Potvin: He took care of everyone. He had to be the toughest, the strongest and the meanest but had a tremendous heart.

Greg Parks: I had known Greg since I was 12 years old. He was one of the toughest individuals that I have ever met. He went beyond expectations. He was funny and witty. He was a guy who lived on the edge of everything. He excelled at every level of hockey. He was an amazing guy.

Advice: Bowling Green hockey has a lasting legacy. It means something when you come to BG to play. It's important to know yourself and have an identity outside of hockey as well. Take your time, be still and listen.

Nelson Emerson #19 Center

Nelson Emerson #19, Center

I grew up in a small town in Canada. Like everyone else, hockey was the sport you played when the weather was cold and the winters were long. If you weren't playing on a team, you were practicing in the driveway or in the basement.

I remember looking up to anyone that played in the NHL. When I was a kid, I used to put on a Toronto Maple Leafs jersey and stand in front of the TV for the national anthem. I imagined myself as one of the players on the ice.

I always admired NHL players Darryl Sittler and Wayne Gretzky. I don't think there will ever be anyone like Gretzky. He was a true professional both on and off the ice.

I didn't know too much about college hockey in the United States until I went to play junior hockey in Stratford, Ontario (Canada) and played for Denis Flanagan. There was a connection because Denis's son, Terry was an assistant coach at BGSU at the time. Stratford does have that connection for sending players to Bowling Green. So, I started thinking that maybe playing college hockey would help me physically, mentally and academically.

Terry Flanagan and Buddy Powers recruited me to play for Bowling Green. They were the first ones who reached out and that was a special feeling. Other schools made offers as well but I had a feeling that BG was the right place to play. I felt comfortable. I have nothing but amazing things to say about this coaching team while I was at BG. Coach York, Coach Powers and Coach Flanagan were amazing together and brought out of us what was needed. Jerry York was like a father figure to many of us. He allowed me to use my skills and I felt I had freedom as a player.

The night we won the CCHA was emotional. I was a freshman at the time so seeing all of the hard work that the seniors and put forth over time was a learning experience. The upper classmen guided us through the critical moment. The fans showed us that Bowling Green was definitely a hockey town. As a player, looking into the stands and seeing the emotions from fans is something I will always remember.

Bowling Green fans always supported the team. We had a Hall of Fame coach, a great team and supportive fans. We were all in this together. Everyone was behind us.

Coach Jerry York is a remarkable person and coach. He was always guiding us the right way. It wasn't all x's and o's on the board. He taught us about life. His influence still stays with me to this day. We were lucky to have him while we were at BG. He and Buddy Powers were an unbelievable combination. They had so much respect for each other.

Remembering Terry Flanagan: It's tough to talk about Terry. He left us at such a young age. He was a great person, understood hockey and formed great relationships with the team. He had a great sense of humor. We wouldn't have been where we were without Coach Flanagan.

Marc Potvin: Marc, Kevin Dahl and I all knew each other from playing at Stratford. Marc's characteristics brought great talent to the team. He was tough. He stuck up for his teammates. He was a terrific person both on and off the ice. He was like a big teddy bear. He was also warm and gentle. He was special to all of us.

Greg Parks: We both played the position of center at BG so we had a little bit of a friendly rivalry. We would challenge each other which made me a better player. He was very competitive and wanted to win. He was critical to our team's success.

I wanted to mention that Scott Slater and his family deserve a lot of recognition for all they have done and contributed to the BG hockey program. BG is the best place to play college hockey.

Advice: Keep your ears open. Pay attention. You have many experienced coaches and players that you can learn from. You have a great opportunity.

An older gentleman once told me to make sure I use hockey but don't let hockey use me. That means you need to take advantage of every opportunity the university has to offer in addition to hockey. Enjoy the ride.

Joe Quinn #20 Right Wing

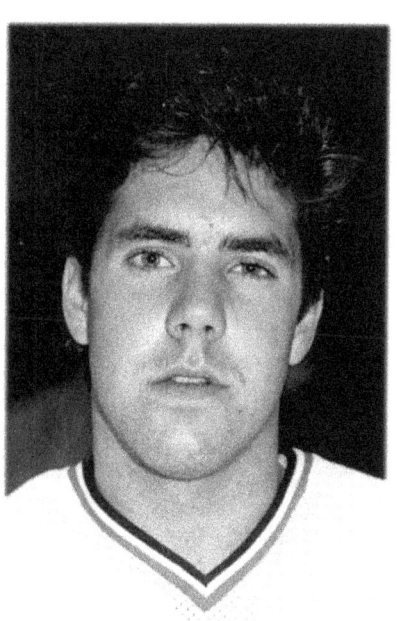

Joe Quinn #20, Right Wing

I grew up in the prairies of Canada so what else was there to do? I am from a family of 12 kids, with the five youngest being boys, so hockey was part of our daily life.

I've always had a love for the game. Two hockey events that really stick out for me and inspired me to play was watching the Canada Summit Series vs. USSR 1972 and the Montreal Canadiens vs. Chicago Blackhawks 1973. My favorite NHL players were Guy Lafleur and Wayne Gretzky. Guy Lafleur was The Flower and Gretzky was The Great One.

I left home at 17 years old to play Junior hockey in British Columbia. I played on three different teams over two years in Junior Hockey to get to BG.

I came down on a site visit in the summer of 1985 before my second year of Junior hockey. I had an ok year in my first year of Junior hockey in British Columbia. It was a quasi-informal visit, as BG had not offered me any scholarship opportunities at that time. Wayne Wilson picked me up at the Toledo airport. I met Terry Flanagan, Buddy Powers and Jerry York at the rink and we all had lunch together later that day. I went to a garage party with Wayne Wilson and met Iain Duncan and a few other players who were attending summer school.

So, without even seeing a practice or a game, I knew I wanted to come to BG. It was based off the people I met on a weekend. Terry Flanagan saw me play in British Columbia during my first year. Buddy Powers and Jerry York saw me play during my second year when I ended up playing Junior hockey again in Calgary, Alberta.

We were fortunate to be in a winning environment, which elevated the bonding between teammates. Nelson Emerson was my roommate for four years and we had a great first year together in the dorm as well as the next three years off campus. Our freshman class included Kevin Dahl, Marc Potvin, Paul Connell, Nelson Emerson and myself.

We were ushered into college hockey with a powerhouse team, with great leadership. I bet I could tell a story about each guy on that team on and off the ice.

I can meet up or reach out to any of the players or coaches from my time period and have a bunch of laughs and a great time. When the opportunity arises, I contact others to see how they are doing. It is just that simple. The older we get, the better we are!

Bowling Green hockey fans are definitely committed. I believe they loved the hockey games more than the players and coaches. It was very special to witness how engaged the fans were, before, during and after the games, through the entire season. Many of us players were on the ice when you could not hear yourself think due to the BG crowd noise. It was an awesome experience.

Jerry York is a very good person, above being a very successful coach. There is no perfect person or process, but the older I get, the more I appreciate what he did for the players on the team. He had to lead over 20 players who were all in their early 20s with many divergent personalities. That was not an easy task but the fact that Coach York was honest and cared for what was the best for the players and program, speaks for itself. For my freshman year, I learned not to be too hard on myself and keep persevering. I had an up and down year on the ice but was proud to have earned a spot on that team.

Remembering Terry Flanagan: He had honesty, integrity and grit which are requirements to be successful in life. He was one of the best humans I ever met. He has been missed.

Marc Potvin: He was a great teammate who could be an intimidating force on the ice. I admired his dedication to improving his skills at practice and impacting the game in different facets. He played the game with intensity. Off the ice, he was kind of larger than life, always there for a good time and quite often the life of the party. His antics are memorable and can make me laugh 35 years later.

Greg Parks: He was the ultimate competitor. His compete level was off the charts. You can't teach what he had. He was "clutch" and played to win. Off the ice, if there was action happening, he was most likely the one stirring the pot. Golf, playing cards or having a good time, he was a catalyst for fun.

If you really look at the success of BG hockey, you may want to look at the people beyond their respective playing time at BG. Look at the NHL, the best league in the world and then look at the players, coaches, management, scouts and media. Look at college hockey and hockey development systems in the U.S. There are so many BG alumni who impact the game at all levels. I would bet BG punches way beyond its weight in all these arenas. I believe it was due to the experience of being at BG, which includes the team, the town and the people.

There were many people in the town of Bowling Green that had a positive impact on many of the players such as Scott Slater, Tom "Doc" Wojciechowski, Al Heringhaus and Bob and Jean Romans.

Advice: Time goes by fast. Be proactive for yourself, but also keep the bigger picture in perspective. Enjoy your experience. You are lucky to play for Bowling Green.

Clarke Pineo #21 Left Wing

Clarke Pineo #21, Left Wing

My older brother was a hockey player so I followed in his footsteps. I wanted to play hockey with my brother. He is five years older than I am and I did everything in my power to keep up with him.

As a child, I always admired Bobby Clarke of the Philadelphia Flyers. Once I became a Don Mills Flyer hockey player, I wore #16 and I was the captain just like Bobby. I thought he was a good leader and tough.

I was fortunate enough to have played with Brian McKee in the Ontario Junior Hockey League (OJHL) and he was a good friend. I had narrowed down my top two schools to attend which were Michigan State or Bowling Green. I chose Bowling Green because I wanted to play with Brian.

It was an amazing experience to play at BG. My teammates were great. Our boosters were amazing. Once I cracked the lineup to play, I was really fired up. Buddy Powers recruited me. I remember my dad and I having dinner with Buddy and talking about playing for BG.

My friendships at BG were priceless. Parksy (Greg Parks) and I remained friends after BG and had some amazing times away from the game with each other and our families.

The night we won the CCHA was a surreal experience. We had an amazing team.

Bowling Green hockey fans and booster families were amazing with their support both on and off the ice. The fans rattled our opponents and fired us up on game nights.

Coach Jerry York and I were a little bit like oil and water to be honest. I was vocal during our coach and player meetings, so it was up to Coach Buddy Powers to take me under his wing.

I learned that I was way too stubborn. Honestly, although I got hurt my second year, I pushed back on going to summer school, which would eventually cost my scholarship.

Remembering Terry Flanagan: He was more of a father figure to me than a coach. Our interactions around the rink were cordial and respectful.

Marc Potvin: He was a great guy and teammate. He had a tremendous work ethic and was a beast in the weight room.

Greg Parks: Words cannot express my respect and admiration for Parksy. We were inseparable on and off the ice. We were the "Pins and Parksy" show. Wherever you saw one of us, the other was right behind at all times.

Advice: Embrace the moment and live each day.

Brian Meharry #22 Center

Brian Meharry #22, Center

My grandmother signed me up for skating class and hockey class when I was just two years old. I really didn't know I was interested in hockey until I started playing.

I'm from Toronto and back then, it was a hockey hot bed. I felt I was a good hockey player. I seemed to play the game well even at a young age. I loved playing.

As far as NHL players, I thought Wayne Gretzky was a Phenom. He was definitely special. I also admired the guys on the Toronto Maple Leafs such as Darryl Sittler and Dave Keon.

I had played for a while with the Toronto Marleys, which was a farm organization of the Maple Leafs so; I was able to practice at Maple Leaf Gardens every Saturday morning.

I remember playing junior hockey in metro Toronto and there were always college scouts in attendance. The team I was playing for was undefeated at the time so all of the players were heavily recruited.

I was offered scholarships at several different colleges. To be honest, Bowling Green was not even on my radar. I had chosen five schools to visit and BG was not one of them. Then as luck would have it, I met Terry Flanagan. I liked him right away. I cancelled my recruiting trip to Ohio State and replaced it with visiting BG. Once I visited the campus, met the team and Coach York, I knew this was the place I wanted to play. If it weren't for Coach Terry Flanagan, I would not have played at BG.

By the time we won the CCHA title, we were among the best league in the country. I was extremely proud of our team. It was very gratifying to win the title. I just wish I could have contributed more to help because I was out of the line up a lot due to a knee injury.

Brian and fellow teammate, Andy Gribble were participants in the hockey movie, "Youngblood" that starred Rob Lowe, Patrick Swayze and Keanu Reeves.

Youngblood was filmed in Toronto and was released in January of 1986. I played right wing on the main line with Rob Lowe and Patrick Swayze played center. Keanu Reeves was the goaltender. Our team's name was the Hamilton Mustangs. Andy Gribble played on the opposing team, which were called the Thunder Bay Bombers. It was a very cool experience.

I never saw an empty seat in the house at the BG ice arena. We may not have had a state-of-the-art arena but we had the best one. That aluminum roof combined with crowds at capacity is a sound I will never forget. There was no better place to play. The interaction between the community, students and players was extremely special.

When I was playing at BG, I thought I knew everything and I didn't really want to learn anything else. But what Coach York taught us definitely showed up later in life. I learned we had better be on time among other things. Everything mattered and it matters today in our everyday lives. He was the best example of integrity. He was teaching us to be men. Coach Buddy Powers was the buffer. We knew the rules. The expectations of us were made clear.

I'm glad I went to Bowling Green where hockey mattered. The town embraced us. We had great leadership in our coaches. We had freedom and yet there was structure.

Remembering Terry Flanagan: He was a Class A human being. He had a wonderful sense of humor. He knew hockey. He came from a legendary hockey family. It was obvious that he was special. He's the reason I came to BG.

Marc Potvin: He was a character. He was funny. He was tough. He would do anything for you. He was a great teammate, a great friend and a great person.

Greg Parks: He was the guy that was stirring it up behind the scenes, on and off the ice.

Bowling Green hockey needs to continue. It needs to be the powerhouse that it once was and be an attraction for the best players.

Advice: Be more mindful of the lessons you are learning. Maximize your amazing opportunities at BG. Lean into your education, leadership, structure and environment. Sometimes that may not sound like fun but if and when the professional hockey career has run its course, you will have other tools to fall back on.

Chad Arthur #23 Left Wing

Chad Arthur #23, Left Wing

I remember watching the Chicago Blackhawks on television when I was a kid. I was very excited about hockey. My dad asked me if I wanted to play and I told him that I would like to try.

Some of the NHL players I admired were Al Secord, Bobby Hull, Bobby Orr and Ken Dryden.

One opportunity led to another and eventually I played for a team called the Chicago Minor Hawks. Mickey Norton was the woman in charge. She started Team Illinois. I actually called her my aunt. She was instrumental in helping to take my hockey career to the next level.

Eventually I was scouted and offered to play at Miami University in Ohio, Bowling Green, Northeastern and Brown Universities. I chose Bowling Green because there were some other guys there from the Chicago area.

I was very fortunate to play at BG. I played with many great players. I remember first meeting Paul Ysebaert and thought that was awesome. The roster for the 1986-1987 season was phenomenal. I loved BG. I thought it was a great university for academics. It definitely was a hockey town. I also have to give mention that going to Mark's and the Brathaus was fun.

I was the jokester to keep the mood light when nerves were starting to take over. Thad Rusiecki was my roommate. We became the best of friends and still are to this day.

The feeling when we won the CCHA title was absolutely euphoric. It was out of control and we loved it. Being with my teammates and celebrating on the ice with each other and the fans was an incredible experience. BG hockey fans are the best.

Coach Jerry York was an incredible and intelligent coach. He knew how to create our lines. He was instrumental and the reason why our team was successful. He made an incredible impact on me personally and professionally. He knew how to utilize all of our talents and his ability to do that was unique. I learned how to dig deep, be a better person and do what you need to do to survive.

Remembering Terry Flanagan: Terry was an incredible person. He was always there for everyone every single day. He went the extra mile. I had known Terry's father, Denis. Losing Terry was tragic. He was a great guy.

Marc Potvin: Marc was one of my best friends. We spent a lot of time together.

Greg Parks: I thought he was a great guy and very talented. He was a unique player. He was shorter than some of the other guys but that didn't stop him. He was phenomenal. We were line mates and sometimes had a love/hate relationship but we were always good friends.

Advice: I would strongly encourage any young hockey player to attend BG. It has a great hockey program and great academics. It's a great college town. You will receive an equal if not better college experience than any other campus.

Iain Duncan #24 Left Wing
Co-Captain

Iain Duncan #24, Left Wing Co-Captain

I first became interested in hockey because of my older brother, Scott. Being Canadian, you have a choice of hockey or hockey as you were growing up. I wanted to be like my big brother. He was always playing hockey in the driveway with his friends.

Darryl Sittler was the captain of the Toronto Maple Leafs and I loved the way he played. When I got a little older, I really admired the way Mark Messier (Edmonton Oilers) could take over a game with his skill on both sides of the puck. I thought Darryl could do almost anything in the game of hockey but fight whereas Mark was the ultimate hockey player; he could do everything on the ice and was very physical as well.

I ended up selecting BGSU after a crazy six to eight months of recruiting from schools across the country. My brother played hockey at the University of Notre Dame. I was aware of the great schools within the CCHA and WCHA. I knew that Bowling Green had a great hockey program and I wanted to be part of it. Buddy Powers and Terry Flanagan were the coaches that recruited me to play at BG.

Bowling Green was already known as an upcoming powerhouse and with Coach Jerry York at the helm; the sky was the limit. I fell in love with the campus and the ice arena on an official recruiting trip. The crowd was crazy. Wisconsin was in town to open the season against the Falcons.

I was a co-captain with Todd Flichel for two years. It was a great experience. The funny thing is that Todd and I were freshman roommates and the Winnipeg Jets drafted both of us in 1983. Being a captain on any team is important but being a captain at a Division 1 University was a great test for me as a leader. You must be willing to do the little things that other players didn't want to do but you take on that responsibility because you're one of the captains. I tried to lead by example on the ice, in the weight room, in the classroom and anything having to do with the team as a leader.

The friendships that you have in college are amazing. When you are coming to a new place in a different country, it can be a little scary at first. But, the way I saw it was that I already had between 20 and 25 new friends who were on the hockey team. I have a special bond with several of the guys going back to the NCAA championship from 1984. The bond seems to get stronger every year.

BG fans are the best in the country. I thought the roof of the ice arena was going to pop off the first time I attended a game as a recruit. The fans were crazy and I loved it.

Coach York was an amazing coach and father figure to all of us in the hockey program. We were guided by the best coaching staff in the country, along with Jerry, Terry, Buddy, and Kevin Mann as our graduate assistant. We were all ready to do whatever our coaches wanted us to do, on the ice, off the ice and in the classroom. Because if you do not keep your grades up, you are not going to be on the team. Coach York is one of the best coaches that I have ever had. He explained exactly how he wanted things to happen during games and practices. The leadership that he showed rubbed off onto his assistant coaches. We would run through a brick wall for those coaches! I learned so much from Coach York about preparing for games to be successful through very hard practices. Thank you, Coach York, Buddy, and Terry for believing in this skinny kid from Toronto.

I learned a lot about myself when I arrived at BGSU in August of 1983. Not only about being successful on the ice but also being successful in the classroom and the weight room. Hard work does pay off!

Remembering Terry Flanagan: Terry was an incredible person first and foremost. He was a great coach and recruiter, very personable and funny as hell! He could talk to anyone and everyone about the sport of hockey.
Terry was an ambassador for BGSU and the hockey grogram. Everyone that knew Terry; loved Terry. He was always around late night with Buddy Powers having a beer or two with us at Mark's Pizza Pub after a big home win.

Marc Potvin: Marc was a great guy and a great teammate.

Greg Parks: Greg was a one-of-a-kind friend and player. He was small in stature but had the heart of a lion. He was so skilled and had the work ethic of a donkey. Greg was a great friend and a great teammate.

Bowling Green hockey does have a rich history. Learning about BG hockey and all the great history it has accomplished over the last 50 years has been amazing. I am really looking forward to seeing where BGSU hockey is going in the next 20 years. My heart would be full of joy if and when BG can make it back to the Frozen Four!

Advice: My advice to any new players coming to play at BG would be to have fun, work hard and listen to your coaches and advisers. They are there to help you.

Thank you to all the great people of whom I have met over the years at BG. Thank you to all my teammates at BG. Bowling Green, Ohio is a special place and BGSU has a special place in my heart. The two go hand in hand with each other. SPECIAL PLACE – SPECIAL PEOPLE.

Steve Dickinson #26 Forward

Steve Dickinson #26, Forward

Since I am from Bowling Green, I used to spend a lot of time at the ice arena when I was a kid. I remember watching players like Mike Liut, Dave Easton, Ken Morrow, Mark Wells and Mike Hartman when they were at practice. Sometimes they would give me their hockey sticks after practice, which was such a thrill. I was a regular figure at the ice arena in those days. Watching them play hockey inspired me to play. As I got older, I had always wanted to play for BG.

Our Bowling Green High School hockey team won the state championship the same year that BGSU won the national championship (1984). I had set the high school career goal scoring record, nationally, that same year. I also appeared in "Faces in the Crowd" in Sports Illustrated Magazine.

After Bowling Green High School, I played for the Stratford Cullitons in Stratford, Ontario (Canada). Stratford was definitely a pipeline to BGSU as far as recruiting hockey players. I had been in touch with Coach York, Coach Powers and Coach Flanagan and was presented with the opportunity to play at BG.

One of the most intriguing things about BG was seeing the line of fans outside and wrapped around the building. Hockey was the biggest thing in Bowling Green and far more successful during the late 70's, 80's and early 90's. BG had always been one of the top teams in the country. It was phenomenal.

Jerry York has proven to be the most elite coach in college hockey. He was adamant in his approach as to how he wanted things done. Obviously, the way he chose to do things was highly successful. I think Coach Powers and Coach Flanagan detailed everything well and were an outstanding coaching team with Coach York.

Remembering Terry Flanagan: Terry was a great recruiter. His father, Denis was the general manager at Stratford where many of us had played.

Marc Potvin: He was a great teammate. Marc was willing to do the "dirty work" for the guys on the ice. He would always back up his teammates. He was a big part of the excitement and fun that was part of BG hockey.

Greg Parks: Greg was tremendous player. He made players around him better. He could dictate how the offense should be run. He may not have been one of the biggest players but his hockey IQ was off the charts. He had an outstanding work ethic and determination.

Advice: I think there are many more opportunities these days in college hockey. Take advantage of those opportunities. If you put in the effort and the time then good things should happen.

Mike Natyshak #27 Right Wing

Mike Natyshak #27, Right Wing

It was just one of those things when you're growing up in Canada. You played hockey. is what you played. When I was a kid, I remember skating on the frozen river near our home with my family and friends. (Belle River, Ontario) Since a hockey stick in a basement corner or garage was as common as a maple leaf in Canada, getting a hockey stick in your hand as a young lad was pretty much normal. One could usually count on finding some hand me down equipment or an old pair of skates from a family member or even a neighbor to get started.

I started playing organized hockey at about five or six years old and was pretty much "hooked" immediately. No hockey penalty pun intended. Like most who play the game, I found it to be fun, fast and challenging. It was a team game, which means you share the experience whether it's win, lose or draw plus all of the emotions of the game among teammates.

Since I often played as a defenseman during minor hockey, I enjoyed watching Bobby Orr (Boston Bruins). Regardless of what position you played as kids, everyone loved to watch him play. I don't want to come off as a hockey historian, yet it's no stretch to say that he was a paradigm shifter. Anyone who knows the game understands how he changed the perception of what a "defensive" position player in hockey could achieve. Not only was he highly skilled, he was extremely tough and a gentleman. Most of hockey's greatest players are like this, superstars that exhibit a combination of exceptional athleticism, mental and physical toughness, humility and gratitude to their teammates and the game.

As an 18-year-old playing on a Windsor (Ontario, Canada) Junior team, things came together and worked out positively for me as hockey player that year. The Windsor team was a very talented team and the coaches allowed us discretion to play outside what would be considered normal defense and offense roles. As a result of my skilled teammates and the green light to offensively engage as a defenseman, I was averaging almost two points per games. The stars aligned well for me that year. I remember scoring a hat-trick during one of the Junior games that the BGSU coaches attended. Looking back now it's almost a false positive since I was never able to achieve that kind of scoring prowess again. I was fortunate to be chosen to the League's All-Star team that year, which put me on the radar for a number of college hockey teams.

Talking about the stars aligning, it was a tradition that the Windsor team would play Bowling Green's club hockey team each year in an exhibition game. What I didn't realize at the time was that my Windsor coaches had called the BG coaching staff before our game and suggested they watch me play. Things worked out for me again, scoring a goal and adding two helpers in that particular game. I also recall trying to hit anything that moved during that game, and a few of the BG Club players looking at me like, "what is up with this guy"? I think the BGSU club team was also told they were NOT to fight any of us, although I'm sure a few of them wanted to. In the end, Jerry York asked to speak with me after the game and it wasn't long after our conversation that I was offered a scholarship and an opportunity to play at BG.

I loved Bowling Green. It's a special place. I have great memories and even more fondness as the years pass. Bowling Green was also close enough to my home in Canada that my family and friends could attend many of the games. This fact grows on me over the years, especially after losing my father a few years ago. I met my future wife and mother to our four children at Bowling Green. Two of our children have since graduated from BGSU. I was full of pride and euphoria the night we won the CCHA title. Clinching the win against the University of Michigan was a great feeling and achievement. We were a confident team, yet the nature of the sport means that confidence needs to meet the challenge all the way to the final horn! We did!

Seeing the fans lined up outside of the "Ice Arena" waiting for the doors to open for the game is a memory I will always cherish. Enroute to the rink, I often saw students in line before the players arrived. I remember consciously appreciating their presence and physical sacrifice during those blistery cold February weekends! Our fans were unbelievable and the whole fan experience was incredible.

I was fortunate to play in many rinks around the country and BGSU fandom during our era was THE best! We worked hard as a team and our fan support was a reflection of our hard work. It was the ultimate positive feedback.

Coach Jerry York was a true gentleman and one of the best coaches that I have ever had. He taught us the practical, tactical and unique ways of being the best hockey player and teammate one could be. Yet, he also was the consummate example of how to conduct oneself outside of the game. He was consistent and successful. He taught us how to be men. He was a problem solver, with a deceptively good sense of humor who enjoyed a creative solution. I remember he gave us an assignment to choose a "word of the day" from the dictionary. This was a way for the team to extend our collective vocabulary from some of the more common not so collegiate (four letter words) a player might use when things didn't go as planned. With Buddy Powers and Terry Flanagan as his assistants, they were an outstanding coaching team. In my book, they were the best college coaching assistants in the country at the time.

Remembering Terry Flanagan: I learned a lot from Terry: humility, dedication and compassion. I loved Terry. He got me through some challenging times. He was my advocate.

Marc Potvin: Marc played through physical pain. He was a motivator. He was dedicated. He was tough on the outside but was really a sweet guy.

Greg Parks: Greg was an intense individual both on and off the ice. Everything he got, he earned. He was a driven competitor.

Advice: Pick a place to play hockey where you feel you belong. You will know. I found that experience by coming to BG. Embrace the BG tradition as a hockey player.

Dan Kwilas #29 Goalie

Dan politely declined an interview for this book, however, he offered one statement...

"They were a great group of guys."

Gary Kruzich #35 Goalie

Gary Kruzich #35, Goalie All-American

My dad is the one who got me started in hockey. I believe I was around two or three years old at the time. I was on my first hockey team by the age of six. I remember after one of our practices, the coach asked who wanted to be a goalie. I raised my hand to volunteer. I wasn't even sure what it meant to be a goalie. My uniform had to be hand made because I was so small.

Billy Smith who was the goalie for the New York Islanders was my idol. If he changed his mask, I'd change my mask. If he swung his stick and got a penalty, then I swung my stick and got a penalty. I looked the part of him. I played the part of him. It was a thrill to finally meet and skate with him.

I had tried out for the Chicago Minor Hawks and made the team. John Starzinski was a coach who believed in me and encouraged me to keep going. Since I was small in stature, I was often told I would not make it to the next level but he was instrumental for me to keep playing.

Coach Buddy Powers had a brother who saw me play in a junior tournament and told Buddy that they needed to get me onboard. BG was looking for a goalie at the time.

Overall, I had at least 41 letters from different schools that wanted me to play for them. I remember visiting Bowling Green with my dad. We attended a game that was BG vs Ohio State. When we walked inside the ice arena, I liked the atmosphere right away. I turned to my dad and said BG is where I'm coming to play. I'm getting chills right now just reliving that experience.

As a goaltender, I loved going into the rinks of opponents and keeping their fans quiet. Save after save and the opposing team's fans have nothing to say.

The night we won the CCHA was controlled chaos. I wish we could go back to those days and show everyone how it's done. The games, the fans and how we did it! That night was a sell out crowd. We were on the ice about 20 minutes or more after the final buzzer. It was one of the best feelings.

Opposing teams hated playing in our arena. It was a beast. It was a glorified dungeon but it was our home. Fans were packed in there from ice level to the roof. It truly was a beautiful sight.

When we were in the locker room, we could hear the crowd. That got you more amped up for the game. BG hockey fans are the greatest and the loudest. Section A should receive a historical plaque to be displayed at the arena. That section needs to go down in history.

You always knew where you stood with Coach York. He was big on values. He was psychologically one of the best coaches that I ever played for. What I learned from him was that people matter. I wish I would have given back more to the community when I played for BG. My time there has turned me into who I am now. There is only one Bowling Green State University.

Remembering Terry Flanagan: He had a wonderful smile. You could have fun with him. He joked around a lot. We all had fun together.

Marc Potvin: He was a great kid. He shot the puck hard and you felt sorry for whoever was on the receiving end.

Greg Parks: He was a fireball. He wasn't much taller than me. He gave 100% of himself all the time.

Bowling Green has had a strong hockey legacy. We have a lot of big names in a lot of big places that came from BG hockey. Everyone needs to bleed the colors of burnt orange and brown and understand the meaning.

Advice: Always have a Plan B. It's important to have a back up plan. Don't rely on only hockey. You will need to have other foundations in place for your future.

Team Support

Scott Slater, Slater Family Ice Arena

My kids played hockey when they were little. All four of my sons played hockey for Bowling Green High School. My two daughters were figure skaters. Overall, we were definitely a hockey family.

During the 1986-1987 season my family was a host family for some of the players. At the time we were hosts for Mike Natyshak. But, we always had some of the other players and their friends over to our home for dinner. Host families provided a sense of home and support for players who were away from their families. Unfortunately, host families are no longer a practice at Bowling Green.

For a period of time, it had appeared as though the university was going to lose the ice arena and the hockey program.

I think some people have given me far too much credit for helping to save the ice arena when things looked to be in jeopardy. We need to acknowledge everyone who participated and have them recognized. Together we kept the ice arena and the hockey program at BG. The ice arena is a gathering space for the community and the heart of BG.

I think education is so important in addition to playing sports. I always tell student athletes to get their education and finish their degrees. It's important to help people connect.

The hockey community in Bowling Green is a family. You live together, you travel together, and you grow together. It's like having an extended family. Players, students and the community create a positive atmosphere together.

Ray Schneider, Professor

Sport Management Program at BGSU
Co-Author with Eddie Powers: "Cavallini from Kane" (2015)

I have been at Bowling Green State University since the fall of 1998 as a professor in the Sport Management program. I knew Bowling Green had a rich hockey history but did not become an actual fan until I arrived in 1998.

Supporters of BG hockey are extremely passionate. Hockey is in the blood of the Bowling Green community and campus. People care about hockey from the youth organization (BG Ice Cats) to the college team. The players, coaching staff and everyone involved are visible and become part of the city.

Ray discusses the book, "Cavallini" from Kane. In 2014, Bob Suter had passed away. He was a member of the Miracle on Ice team. Eddie Powers and I were discussing his loss and decided it was important that we capture the memories from those that were involved in the 1984 BGSU Hockey National Championship. Eddie has been a wonderful friend. We had a wonderful time writing about the 1984 team.

I think Jerry York is the greatest hockey coach. More impressively, one of the kindest people I have ever met.

Buddy Powers played the role of assistant coach very well. It wasn't easy during the 1980s to balance and support the head coach and players. Buddy was a pro at everything.

Unfortunately, I never had the privilege to meet Terry Flanagan but I learned about him from the 1984 team while writing the book. It was clear he was a mentor and friend to all who knew him.

BG hockey has an incredible history. People want to see the program get back to winning conference championships and competing in the NCAA tournament.

Dr. Tom Wojciechowski
"Doc Wojo"
Team Doctor

(L to R) Iain Duncan, Doc Wojo, Todd Flichel

Doc Wojo (Dr. Tom Wojciechowski), Team Doctor

I grew up during the 1950s in Toledo. My mom would take my brothers and I to hockey games. I used to follow a team called The Toledo Mercurys. My mom was a big hockey fan. But oddly enough, I never learned to skate. My sons, Tom and Edward played youth hockey at the ole Toledo Sports Arena.

In June of 1978, I moved to Bowling Green. Interestingly, when the BGSU hockey team won the national championship in 1984, my son Tom was playing at Bowling Green High School and their team won the state championship. Plus, figure skater Scott Hamilton, who was from Bowling Green, Ohio, won a gold medal in the 1984 Olympics! 1984 was quite the year for Bowling Green!

I had become acquainted with a doctor who was the team doctor for The Toledo Goaldiggers. He suggested that maybe I could help on weekends and he would cover the games during the week. So, I worked with The Toledo Goaldiggers for a little over two years as kind of an associate assistant.

I am sure the readers will find this next story somewhat amusing. Before I became the team doctor for the BGSU hockey team, there was another doctor serving in that role. However, he was a gynecologist. He said he really wasn't qualified to be in sports medicine. Shortly thereafter, I became the team's doctor. I've been the Falcon hockey team's doctor for over 40 years. I love it.

I always felt BG hockey fans were rabid. I remember students standing outside waiting to come in for the game. There was always such tremendous support from the community and from the students.

Jeff Weiss, Statistician

My parents moved to Bowling Green in 1973 and that's when I started going to hockey games. My dad had two season tickets. One night he would take my mom. Another night he would take my brother or me. I remember seeing BG greats such as George McPhee, Mark Wells and Ken Morrow when I was a kid. Seeing them play started my path to become a hockey fan.

When I was in junior high I had met the Sport Information Director at BGSU. Through him, I was able to start out by helping in the basketball press box at BG. By the time I was in high school, Bowling Green started the Sport Management Program. I had visited other universities but BG seemed like a good fit. When I was a freshman, I started doing stats for the hockey team during the 1983-1984 season.

I was the person keeping track of what is called a "shot chart". I recorded information on any player that shot the puck from either team. I wrote down the player's jersey number and what was the result of that shot whether it be a goal, a save, blocked by a defenseman and so forth. I had a blank sheet of the ice rink where I would record my information.

The Bowling Green hockey fans are what made the games fun. It was always a blast listening to the Bleacher Creatures in Section H.

After the games, I would go into the locker room to give the stats to the coaches. One-night Gary Kruzich (goalie) asked me how many saves he had because he was certain it was least 35. I told him it was 25 saves. Then he went into "Gary-mode" and chased me around the locker room with his hockey stick! The good ole days!

Coaches Jerry York, Buddy Powers and Terry Flanagan created a culture for the team. Everyone knew their role and did it well. I feel very fortunate to have been at BG during such a great time for hockey.

Angela Gorgone Swartz, Statistician/Videographer

From the time I was five years old, my dream was to work in the NHL. I wanted to be the GM of the New York Rangers. My reason for attending Bowling Green was twofold. First, they were one of only a handful of colleges that had a Sport Management Program. Second, they had a top-notch Division I hockey team that had won the NCAA. So, BG was the only school that had both requirements. George McPhee was my favorite Ranger and I knew he went to BG as did Ken Morrow of the New York Islanders.

My freshman year was the fall of 1985. My intentions were to try and get a job doing stats or something with the team. I saw an ad in the BGSU newspaper that read "Meet the BGSU Hockey Team" dinner. I bought a ticket and introduced myself to Coach York. I told him of my interest to perhaps work for the team in some capacity. He told me they needed a statistician to keep track of the face-offs, hits, chances and giveaways during games and asked if I would be interested. I told him I would be interested and there was a press pass waiting for me for the upcoming game. My official job was statistician and videographer during practices. My unofficial job was typing their school papers! I was there until December of 1988 when I left to do my internship for the New Jersey Devils.

There is such a storied history with so many great hockey players from BG that went onto the NHL. This was at a time when college hockey players moving into the NHL was not mainstream.

BG hockey fans are passionate, fun, loyal and extremely knowledgeable about hockey. I really believe the hockey team brought the community together as well as the university. The team was definitely treated like rock stars.

I couldn't have been more blessed to have had the opportunity to know this group of men. Some of my fondest, most treasured memories are working for this hockey team. You become like a family. I never had any brothers so these guys were like my brothers. I felt they were my friends. The coaches were just as wonderful. They were always available to chat; the door was always open which meant a lot to me when you are over 600 miles away from home. If they hadn't given me the opportunity to work with this team, I'm not sure my journey to work within the NHL would have transpired. I cannot begin to express my gratitude.

I loved all the guys on the team but I had close friendships with Paul Connell, Al Leggett, Todd Flichel, Greg Parks, Andy Gribble, Brent Regan and Scott Paluch.

Coach York was a class act all the way. He was a "player's coach". You could tell the players enjoyed playing for this coaching team of York, Powers and Flanagan.

Remembering Terry Flanagan: I was intimidated a bit by Terry at first. Initially I thought he was kind of gruff but quickly learned that he was one of the nicest, funniest humans around. Something was always missing after he passed.

Marc Potvin: He was one of the most genuine and funniest human beings I have ever known. No one could make me laugh like Marc. I can't even remember a time that he wasn't smiling or joking. He was fiercely competitive on the ice and very tough.

Greg Parks: Greg was another one near and dear to my heart. He may have been one of the smaller guys on the team but had the heart and determination of someone twice his size. He always had a funny joke. I remember he used to try and get me to increase his face-off numbers!

During my time at BG, I learned life is what you make it and tomorrow isn't promised. I knew what I wanted to do at an early age and was determined to make it happen. Sometimes if you want something bad enough, you need to take risks. Watching this team compete day after day and seeing the support they afforded one another was an inspiration for me to work harder.

Don "Woody" Woods, Equipment Manager

Don "Woody" Woods, Equipment Manager
By Kristen Woods-Batcho, written in memory of her father Don Woods

My father was Don Woods. He was the equipment manager. He was the team's first equipment manager when hockey was added to the university in 1969. He started in 1969 and retired in 1996. He was the team's only equipment manager until he retired.

I think there were many things that dad liked about his job. He was proud of his craft. Skates had to be perfectly sharpened, uniforms had to be perfectly laundered and fixed. Sticks had to be perfect, and while the players taped their sticks, he made sure when the batch of sticks came in for each player that the sticks were perfect. I remember him showing me where the extra sticks were kept. He knew everything about each player and their stick preference. The knowledge he had and remembered about players even years after players left BGSU was remarkable.

Dad also liked seeing so many players walk through the locker room door as cocky, know-it-all, young teens and walk out the doors as grown young men. He knew that he helped to shape and influence the person they became when they left BGSU. Don't get me wrong, there were many players that drove dad nuts, especially as the generations changed and transitioned through the locker room doors. But, he didn't put up with any nonsense. He made sure players knew the rules of the locker room and that the rules were followed. He ran a tough, tight ship in the locker room, but he always knew it was in their best interest not to be treated like babies or coddled.

Dad really liked building relationships with the players. He started the HOGO (Hockey Old-Timers Golf Outing) in 1983 to bring former players, student managers, and coaches together for a weekend of golf, friendship, and shenanigans. It brought him joy to bring everyone together to reconnect and reminisce about the good old days. He spent countless hours mailing out registration forms, organizing the returned forms into three-ring binders (aka the "Bible"). He would gripe when someone would tell him they were coming but he hadn't received their registration form or their money yet. He would get upset when he would receive "return to sender" mail because the person hadn't told dad they had moved.

The first thing that comes to mind about a BG Hockey fan is loyalty. Loyal through the good times and the bad times. BG hasn't won a National Championship in 40 years and yet people still go to the games and support the team. They just want the team to be the best it can be.

For students, it was crazy! I remember as a young girl, when the doors would open, seeing the students come running into the arena and jumping over the bleachers to get to their favorite seat. Tradition still rings through the building with the "Who's He – Nobody" when the opposing starting lineup is introduced. The students still heckle the opposing team, and now my daughter is one of those hecklers.

Being a BG hockey fan is almost like a Shakespeare play – full of emotions, tragedy, triumph, joy and sorrow. For me, personally, my perspective of being a fan has changed throughout the years. I was a very young child enamored with the players. Then I attended BGSU and was friends with the players. Now I watch hockey through my "Bleacher Creature" daughter's eyes. I am proud of my hometown and alma mater team. I will always be a BG Hockey fan.

There is such a rich, strong history of the hockey program that makes it so important to the university and community. And again, it goes back to relationships. There were families in the community who would host/sponsor a player and be like their parents away from home. Community members went to the games not only to support the team but also to support "their" player. It's the relationships that brought the community and university together.

Slater Ice Arena is a special place to bring the community together. Not only by housing BGSU hockey, but BGHS hockey, youth hockey, figure skating, learn-to-skate, summer camps, BGSU physical education classes, curling, etc. It was the place to be when there was a home hockey game. For me, personally, it was also the place to be during the summer. I'd go to work with dad, spend the day figure skating and then go home with him at the end of the day.

Dad had a tradition of putting on his skates and going out to practice when a particularly important series weekend coming up. He didn't say much, but everyone knew when he strapped on the skates that it was a big weekend and they needed to win.

Rob Schaad, Student Equipment Manager

My freshman year at Bowling Green was in the fall of 1987. My original plan was to become an Athletic Trainer. I had changed my major a couple times and finally graduated with a Bachelor of Arts in Independent Planned Program – History of Sport.

I am from Mansfield, Ohio so I did not have a lot of exposure to hockey. I do recall watching the 1980 Winter Olympics and the Miracle on Ice but that was all.

I worked with the hockey team my freshman year as a Student Athletic Trainer and thought it was a lot of fun. My best friend was one of the Student Equipment Managers. I served as a Student Equipment Manager under Don Woods from 1990 through 1996.

I think BG hockey fans are wonderful. It was fun being at home games and hearing them "bring the noise". Once I started working with the team it was an awesome experience to see and hear the fans from the bench.

The Bowling Green hockey community is amazing. The Slater Arena is a community focal point in the winter and while it is one of the older arenas in the country, it is still maintained at the highest level.

Coach York was a great person and coach. It was only after he left Bowling Green and returned to his alma mater at Boston College that I truly was able to reflect and appreciate all of his work and dedication.

Remembering Terry Flanagan: I only knew Terry a short time before he passed away. He was a brilliant tactician and was always friendly.

Marc Potvin: Marc was an awesome guy. He gave me my nickname of "RobBob". I remember he came back after we graduated for one of the golf outings and it was like time had stood still. We talked and reminisced as though we never left BG.

It has been a true honor and privilege to be part of the BG hockey program. While I was not a player, I felt I was just as much a part of team and my role with them.

Thank you for considering me for this book project. While I arrived to the program after the 1986-1987 season, I still have great memories of the players. I worked for Don Woods and also with Bill Jones who were a big part of the 1986-1987 season and were huge influences. Bill Jones, the Head Athletic Trainer for BG at the time was the main reason I chose to attend BG. Don "Woody" Woods was the program's first Equipment Manager. He was like a second dad to me and I learned "the ropes" from him.

Jeff Shell, Referee

Jeff Shell, Referee

I played hockey all the way through high school. My older brother was playing at Michigan State. He got into refereeing while at MSU and suggested I get involved as well. I thought it sounded like fun. The first thing I did was to register with the American Amateur Hockey Association. My brother and I would referee together. We started refereeing the little mite's hockey games, then I was able to referee where I went to college.

I became a referee in the CCHA league in 1983. I had a great career as a referee that lasted over twenty years. I worked with many different hockey leagues. In addition to having excellent skating ability, you also need to have a feel for the game and have rapport with the players.

You have to remember the heat of the battle during games. Tensions run high, tempers become shorter and you need to keep it together because you are there to guide. I never embarrassed a player or a coach. You give penalties to players so they realize what the limits are and they need to play within those limits.

I think the referees and linesmen make up the third team on the ice. We support each other and look out for player safety.

Conflict on the ice can be real or perceived. Players are intense and they play with that intensity. They earned their ice time. You have to treat them with respect. You work to turn down the heat after the whistle especially if the players are in front of the net. I would have conversations with players but, if they screamed and flailed their arms in my face, the interaction was over.

Bowling Green was one of my favorite places to referee. I never had any conflicts with Coach Jerry York. He, Buddy Powers and Terry Flanagan were absolute professionals. They were true ambassadors for the game. Referees were treated well at BG and that included the community as well as the university.

I remember the lady that sat near the penalty box area and she always had a Falcon puppet. I enjoyed seeing the fans holding up the newspapers before the game started. There was a great deal of tradition for BG hockey games. I always thought it was a great place.

During the 1986-1987 season, I was a referee at BG ten times. My brother was also a referee a few times at BG as well. I was always glad to see BG on my schedule. I knew Paul Ysebaert personally. He had an extremely high hockey IQ. He played hard. He was a super player.

Todd Flichel was an absolute giant. He was a big guy but never a bully. He was a great leader.

Iain Duncan was a tremendous skater. He was a leader. He worked hard and always seemed to be on the edge. He definitely racked up penalty minutes. He was hard-nosed and did whatever it took to get the job done.

Nelson Emerson was a consummate professional. He was a coach's player.

Brian McKee usually had a jab or a comment then gave a smile. He was a great player.

Gary Kruzich was a wildman!

The entire team was highly skilled and talented. It was a reflection of the coaching staff.

Dennis Parish, Referee

I started refereeing during my last year of playing junior hockey. I started refereeing around the city of Detroit. I earned $7.50 per hour. This was around 1967. I would be paid two extra dollars if I was willing to break up fights in the parking lot.

I ended up going to a referee school in Canada. I had worked for other leagues but I loved the CCHA league the best.

Hockey referees need to have humility. You need to understand the difference between being cocky and being humble.

Referees have to be great communicators. If you are a competent official then the coaches you work with will feel confident in their own game plan because they know the officials will do what is needed.

You let the hockey game come to you. A referee does not jump in and dictate the tone. It's up to each team to set the tone. You have an understanding that emotions and tempers are elevated but a referee needs to keep it together and remain impartial. There always needs to be an understanding of the teams, their history together, player rivalry and more.

Jerry York is a quality person. One of the finest gentlemen I have ever met. The quality of players he has had over the years speaks to his leadership.

Jim Sibeto, Student Equipment Manager

My major at Bowling Green State University was Sport Management and Sport Marketing and Public Relations. I was working with Joe Sharp as a student equipment manager when he told me that Don "Woody" Woods needed a student equipment manager for the hockey team. The rest is history.

BG has such a rich hockey history for producing several players that went onto the NHL. In my eyes, BGSU became famous on the hockey map after winning the NCAA title in 1984.

BG hockey fans are known for their passionate support and strong sense of community. They were very dedicated and provided a lively and energetic atmosphere. The night the team won the CCHA title, I felt excitement, pride and a sense of accomplishment for players, coaches, fans and the entire community.

Coach York was a pivotal figure during this era. His leadership and philosophy helped to shape BG hockey. He has become one of the most successful coaches in college hockey history.

Remembering Terry Flanagan: Terry was highly respected for his knowledge of the game and mentoring of players. Everyone who knew him and benefited from his coaching will always remember him fondly.

Marc Potvin: He was a great figure in the world of hockey. He was known for his skill and tenacity. He made significant contributions to the team's success. Marc made us laugh all the time. He was truly an inspiration.

Greg Parks: Greg was a leader. He exemplified the qualities of dedication, teamwork and perseverance. His memory lives on as a symbol to the excellence of BG hockey. What I learned for life during that time were resilience, dedication, discipline, community and support.

Rhonda Albers as Frieda Falcon

Rhonda Albers, Frieda Falcon

1983 was my freshman year. I was in the BGSU marching band when I first met Freddie and Frieda Falcon when they visited our band camp. I actually thought they were very cool and wondered how they got to dress up in furry suits.

As I remember, there was no specific requirement for being a mascot. Many of the "Freddie and Frieda Falcons" came from the BGSU marching band. I enjoyed listening to the crazy adventure stories from the others and I stored that in my mind for future reference.

I was also part of Section A at hockey games. Section A was a very boisterous and involved student section at the ice arena. The ice arena was another home for Freddie and Frieda Falcon.

Training to be a mascot was trial by fire. At the time, there was not any formal training. Any advice came from former "birds" who had played the role. We were pretty much given free reign and reminded not to get into trouble.

Over the generations, Freddie and Frieda Falcon have carved their place into BGSU lore. The Alpha Phi Omega guys (Norbert Billing, Hugh Simmonds and Fred Frisbie) who first wore the suit developed the personalities and representation for the university in so many ways.

During my time at BG, Freddie and Frieda Falcon were expected to cover all home varsity football games, men's and women's basketball games and hockey games.

I started mascot appearances at the new student registration. I showed up in dining halls and tried to serve food behind the counter. I walked through men's residence hall floors. I left gum in open cash register tills. I "stole" golf carts and went for joyrides. I wandered through all the offices on campus including the athletic offices and the campus president.

I sat at tables and put my feet up on desks. I left gum and smiles for everyone I could reach. I loved giving high fives, hugs and beak kisses. Everyone may not have appreciated my shenanigans but, there were very few complaints.

As years, seasons and events have progressed, so have Freddie and Frieda's participation in non-athletic events. They have become such a big part of the lifeblood at BGSU that their presence is expected everywhere.

I really enjoyed the one-on-one interactions. I loved getting little kids to shake my hand, ring the cowbell or take a piece of bubble gum from my hand. I loved approaching a random person and having a "conversation".

BGSU was the first place I saw hockey at any level. I was a fan at the first whistle. Friends in the hockey band explained the game and taught me the group heckles and chants. I lived for hockey games. It was a bonus to be in the hockey band and not have to buy a ticket. Because of my dedication to the hockey band, I was invited to travel to Lake Placid for the 1984 NCAA finals with the BGSU hockey team and the band.

Freddie and Frieda led the hockey team onto the ice at home games. We were not proficient skaters, were in large costumes, and could not see very well. So, while we always had a presence, we stayed out of the way. The hockey team was always protective of us when opponents were also on the ice. They let us know how much they appreciated our presence.

My husband, Eric Albers, was Freddie Falcon in 1984 and traveled with the team to Lake Placid for the NCAA championship. He is often invited to team reunions and is pulled into the team photo. Through participation with him and these events, I have another view on how much Freddie and Frieda Falcon are appreciated by the athletes.

I love every last one of the Bowling Green hockey fans. Even the little rink rats (youth hockey boys) who would pull my tail and try to steal gum. They continue to be some of the most passionate fans.

I remember Section A with their group chants and heckles could even be heard over radio broadcasts. They were all clean, funny, creative and very dedicated to BG hockey. Sometimes they would have the players laughing who were trying to hide it from Coach York, who did not seem amused. They would also pick on opposing players to the point there they would lose their focus of the game. Section A taught me how to be a fan.

BG hockey fans remain as passionate as they have ever been. The sounds have changed, the uniforms have changed but the passion and spirit are still in full force.

Janice Schriner, Frieda Falcon

I was a cheerleader for BGSU and unfortunately blew my knee out. I was on crutches and could not continue with try-outs. So, then I decided it might be fun to be Frieda Falcon.

There was not any special training to be Frieda Falcon. However, I do recall being asked if I could ice skate and I said I knew how even though I had never been on skates in my life. The first time I was on skates was when I was Frieda at a hockey game. As I was trying to skate around the arena, a player from the opposing team used his stick to knock my skate out from under me. The fans booed him and I ended up bleeding all over the ice. I actually thought it was funny. I had to make up a story about the cut on my knee to tell my friend. All to protect my identity as Frieda. It made it a very memorable first skate.

Everyone seemed to be happy when they saw Freddie and Frieda Falcon. They brought spirit and cheer to the campus, and still do.

We all loved hockey and were very proud of our team.

Dave Shilling as Freddie Falcon

Dave Shilling and Rhonda Albers

Dave Shilling, Freddie Falcon

My freshman year at Bowling Green was in 1982. It always seemed that whoever was one of the mascots was also a member of the marching band.

Attending hockey games is where I would see "Freddie Falcon" do his stunts and interactions. So, I decided I wanted to be a mascot, too. It looked like fun and I wanted to be part of the chaos. My college roommate was Eric Albers and he was Freddie Falcon for the 1983-1984 season when the hockey team won the national title. (NCAA) I was a mascot at BG for just one season. (1986-1987)

Mascots were allowed to take a basic ice-skating class for free. I could skate but I did take the class and my mechanics improved. Wayne Wilson taught the class. Jim Sibeto who was the hockey team's equipment manager took the class, too. He had no idea I was Freddie Falcon.

I would usually skate out onto the ice first. Then the players would take the ice. I always tried to stay in front of Gary Kruzich (goalie) so I wouldn't get steam rolled. I loved interacting with the crowd and helping to lead cheers.

It was difficult at times to breathe in the Falcon suit. It was wicked hot. There was a lot of fluid loss. I remember weighing myself at a basketball game. I had lost ten pounds of water during the first half of the game.

Freddie and Frieda Falcon are such a huge part of tradition at BGSU. They make people smile and laugh. Back then we did around 100 appearances per year. These days they do about 600 appearances and there are three sets of Freddie and Frieda Falcons. Times have changed!

Whenever I had free time, I would put the suit on and walked around campus to interact with staff and students. If you were wearing the Freddie suit, you could pretty much get away with anything. Bowling Green hockey fans were obnoxious in a very good way. They were incessant. BG hockey is phenomenal.

Dave Kuhar as Freddie Falcon

Dave Kuhar, Freddie Falcon

I remember seeing Freddie Falcon when I was a freshman at BG. It just seemed like a fun thing to do. I knew Eric Albers who was Freddie Falcon in 1984. That was the year the hockey team won the NCAA.

I saw an ad in the BG News that applications were being taken for mascots. I filled out an application and as they say, the rest is history. You're usually a mascot for one year. I was Freddie for the 1986-1987 season.

I knew how to ice skate so I was comfortable on the ice. I had the most fun being Freddie Falcon at hockey games. The acoustics were loud in the ice arena so it was always fun to get the crowd amped up.

I loved putting on the mascot suit and goof off on campus. One of my favorite things to do was harass the campus tour groups. I knew their schedule and the tour guides always took the groups to the same places. I would jump down from trees in front of them or pose as though I was a Greek statue. It was fun.

Freddie and Frieda Falcon are part of the identity of BGSU and are unique to the campus.

I loved BG from the first day I toured the campus which was a windy day in the winter.

I was part of the pep band for hockey games but I loved being Freddie Falcon. It was great to get fans going. I am proud of BG. I am proud to have been Freddie Falcon.

Tom Glick, Announcer

As I tried to scan my 80-year-old memory or what is left of it, I came up with a little tidbit you might find useful.

As we know, there was a player on that team named Paul Ysebaert. Well as was my usual routine at the beginning of each season, I would meet with the hockey Sports Information Director and go over the pronunciations of the new players. Then we would ask each new player to pronounce his name for me. So, after agreeing on Ysebaert with the "t" silent I proceeded to embellish it by saying "eeeez bear" into the microphone! That's how we proceeded through the season.

His second season came around and I continued with the same pronunciation. The fans seemed to love it and I thought Paul did, too. About midway through season two, after the starting lineups were announced I was visited by the hockey Sport Information Director. He informed me that Paul's grandmother was in attendance and she was shocked with my pronunciation! She said his name was pronounced "Eyes-a-Bart"! We then agreed that we should refer to him as his grandmother reported. And so, ended "eeeez bear" and forever more moving forward we called him "Eyes-a-Bart".

Scot Bressler, Assistant in Athletic Business Affairs
Director of Ticket Operations

I was primarily in charge of the ticket sales to all athletic events and assisted in the Athletic Business Office and the Falcon Club which was the fundraising office for the Athletic Department.

Bowling Green has a rich tradition in college hockey. It has been especially exciting and enjoyable for me because I have watched BG hockey since its inception. I remember attending the games when I was a kid.

Hockey gives the university national recognition and attention. It provides something for the community to rally around and support.

Having watched the program from the public view as well as "behind the scenes" view made the CCHA win even more enjoyable. I felt an increased appreciation for the team than the average fan. Getting to know the coaches and players personally added to the excitement.

Both the coaches and players were hard working. There was no one better than Jerry York. He was an excellent coach and an even better person. He was a great family man. He never made anything about himself. He had a sign in the locker room that said, "The name on the front of the jersey means more than the name on the back."

Remembering Terry Flanagan: Terry was special. We were in graduate classes together and got to know each other well. He spent two or three Thanksgiving holidays with my family. We became good friends.

Marc Potvin: Marc was a fun person to get to know. I remember he came over to my house with a few of the other guys to have a meal, hang out and just to get away from things for a while.

During that time at BG, I was still transitioning from a student employee to having a professional career in the Athletic Department. It gave me a great start in learning how to work with people and be professional.

Todd Parker, Friend/Fan

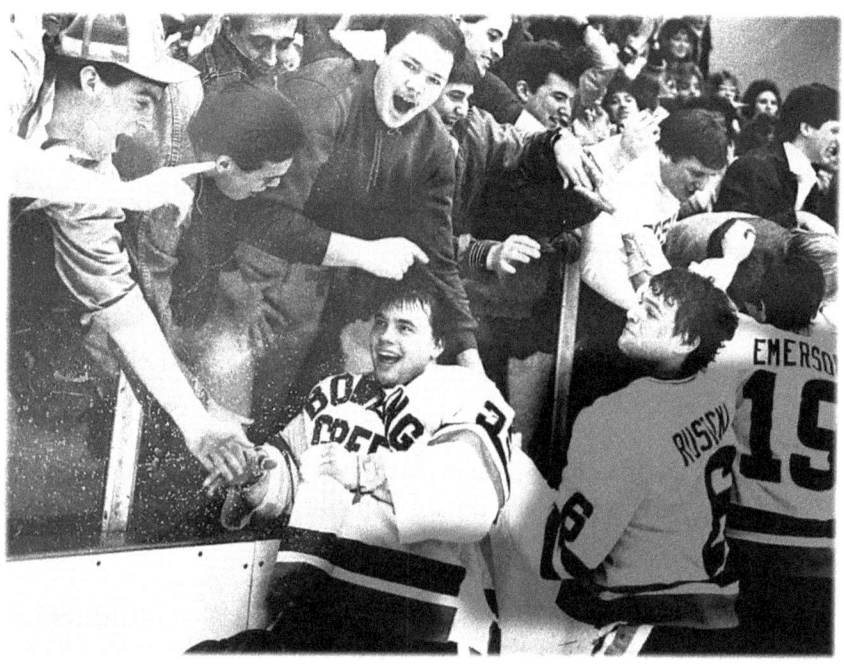

*Todd Parker far left wearing the ball cap after the final buzzer
Celebrating the CCHA title win with players and fans.
BGSU Ice Arena
February 21, 1987*

Todd Parker, Friend/Fan

Growing up in Rochester, New York, I was a huge Boston Bruins fan and loved Bobby Orr. The only problem was that hockey was not on television back then.

BG hockey was on my radar in 1980 because Ken Morrow was in the Olympics. I was actually in Lake Placid the day we beat the Russians in the 1980 Olympic Gold medal game. The national championship in 1984 at BG got me even more interested. It seemed as though every guy on the team was already drafted by an NHL team. It was so much fun following guys like Ysebaert, Emerson and Dahl.

BG hockey fans are the smartest fans in the land. I believe from the fall of 1985 to the spring of 1989 saw some of the best years of hockey talent that came through Bowling Green.

There isn't that much going on in Bowling Green, Ohio therefore BG hockey is great entertainment. It's on the national level and can compete with anyone in the country.

The photo captures the feelings and emotions the night we won the CCHA title. I think I only missed one game the entire season. Winning that title meant that we were better than Michigan State and Michigan, which was a big deal. I met Gary Kruzich (goalie) four years ago at a game and told him I still had this picture. He remembered the exact spot it was taken.

I knew Kevin Dahl and Marc Potvin a little. My friend, Bruce Kratt was roommates with them. I would often get tickets from them so that my parents could sit behind the team bench and not have to wait in line for seats. Going out to Mark's Pub after the Saturday games was the best. Talking with the players was such a thrill. We even got to know a couple of the referees if they stopped at Mark's.

It was a great time for Bowling Green hockey.

Gene Hicks, Friend/Fan

We became a host family to the hockey team by chance. My son Andy was playing hockey and we started attending the games at BG because of his interest. We would stay after games so Andy could meet some of the players. We met Gary Kruzich and he introduced us to some of the other players. We had Gary's parents over to our home a few times. It just took off from there and my family became more involved with the team and hosting some of the players.

During the 1986-1987 season, we mainly hosted Gary Kruzich and Paul Connell. We also got to know some of the other players such as Thad Rusiecki and Chad Arthur. It was a really special time for us as a family and we were proud to be part of the team's journey.

BG hockey fans were incredible during that time. There was so much community support and the arena was always full. It was hard to get seats unless you reserved them. The momentum of the team really brought the community together and it was an exciting atmosphere.

Coach Jerry York was a disciplined and understanding coach. He was easy to talk to and expected the best out of his players. He was also compassionate which made him a great leader. He always engaged with fans and the community.

Remembering Terry Flanagan: Terry had a quiet presence. He took care of business but kept himself out of the limelight. He was always willing to talk about a game and was very nice.

Marc Potvin: He was a physical player, a real workhorse on the ice. He was someone you didn't want to face in the corners because he would usually come out on top. He was a go-getter, always hustled and he played with a lot of heart. He was a force to be reckoned with.

Greg Parks: He was a consistent player and someone you could always depend on. He was skilled with the puck and had hockey smarts. He was the kind of player who had great awareness on the ice, always making the right plays. His presence on the ice was something special.

Hockey is important to Bowling Green because it brings the community and the university together. It's a common interest that bridges the gap between the residents and the students. For the younger kids, it's a source of inspiration. I know my son Andy started playing hockey after he saw the team at BG. It is something that connects everyone and creates a shared sense of pride and excitement.

I would just like to add that the players do not often realize the effect they have on young kids. College athletes can be real role models and their influence can stick with a kid for a life time. Seeing how the community came together to support the team and how it impacted my own family is something I will always cherish.

Beth Burkett, Friend/Fan

My first BG hockey game was in 1978, when my older brother Tim was a student at BG. Wow! What an experience. I don't remember much about the actual game. What I do remember is how crazy the students were at the game: the chants, cheers, and wild celebrations. That one game made me want to be a part of the hockey experience when I arrived at BG as a student.

The 1983-1984 season when I was a freshman was an exciting season. I was late for many of my English classes because of waiting in line at Anderson Arena to get tickets for the weekend games. By the end of the season, I was sleeping overnight at Anderson so I was guaranteed a ticket. We know that season ended with a national championship. I was a devoted fan from then on.

BG hockey fans are devoted to the team and aren't afraid to show it. They are there at every game cheering on the team and continuing the many traditions that have been around since those beginning years.

We all know the cold winters in BG but that doesn't stop the fans from arriving at least two hours before the puck drops just to make sure they get a seat for the game. I remember many cold Friday and Saturday nights waiting outside for the doors to open. Even now when I attend a game, I get to the arena at least 60 minutes before they open the doors to ensure I get to sit in my favorite seat. Thank goodness now, my wait is in the lobby and not outside. I feel the BG fans took it to the next level when they fought along with alumni to keep the hockey program from being cut from the BG sports program. It was "game on" for all of us to do what we could so the "Madhouse on Mercer" would be a permanent fixture on campus.

I have been a BG hockey fan for the past 46 years. I really don't know what it is like to not be a fan. Hockey season is my favorite season of the year. It's wearing BG hockey attire every weekend even if you can't attend the game. It is downloading all the hype videos and watching them over and over. It is introducing new people to BG Hockey so they know what it is really like to a true devoted fan. I know I have brought close to a dozen people to a BG game. Before the game is over, they are begging me to bring them to another game.

There are so many decorations: BG hockey banners, pennants, hockey sticks, pucks, player trading cards and hockey signs in general. I display them in my first-grade classroom. My students read hockey themed books and watch the hype videos every Friday. We sing Ay Ziggy Zoomba in my classroom more than our school's fight song. It is getting kids excited about the game of hockey and wanting to play the game. In the last six years, I have had five students who have ended up joining a hockey team!

The hockey program brings people together and brings fans back to BG. Fans talk about the team and that brings more attention to the university as a whole. When we are supporting the university, we are supporting the community financially as well.

The ice arena holds many fond memories for me. It is where I was introduced to the sport that I fell in love with. It is where I got to have fun and celebrate team victories and championships. It is where I met George McPhee, Doc Emrick, Mark Wells and Scott Hamilton. It is where my son, Nathan learned how to skate and in his junior year of high school, where he played one of his hockey games with the Fremont Ice Wolves. People have teased me that it is my home away from home. I would have to agree because it is like home. I can't imagine BG hockey not being a part of my life.

My favorite players of the 86-87 Season were Mike Natyshak, Todd Flichel, Scott Paluch, Rob Urban, Don Barber, Nelson Emerson, Brent Regan and Iain Duncan. Coach York was the best hockey coach. What a class act. He always put the team and players first and his own accomplishments and honors as secondary. That resulted in the team's success.

LeeAnn Rasey, Friend/Fan

My first experience with BG hockey was when my cousin Eric, a BG student, took us to a game. The whole arena was cheering. The organ was playing. Players were moving fast on the ice. The atmosphere was exciting! Then we met Beth Burkett who was already a huge hockey fan and the three of us made home hockey games a weekend priority! The fans were so into it. The arena would go crazy!

When the team was on the road, we listened to the game on the radio.

Back in the day, we waited outside at the door, getting ready to run to our spot in the ice arena. Meanwhile, we saw the guys pull up in their cars all dressed up in their suit and tie. You can't get more exciting than that!

It was a very exciting place and everyone there was there for the same thing, which was a thrilling hockey experience! The atmosphere of everyone cheering, clapping and everyone shouting, "WHO'S HE? NOBODY!" while we were holding our newspapers as the opposing team was introduced.

Some of my favorite players in those days were Brian McKee, Brent Regan, Scott Paluch, Paul Ysebaert, Todd Flichel and Gary Kruzich.

Attending hockey games helped to make my time at BG memorable. We still talk about those days!

Bruce Kratt Friend/Fan

I remember being a student fan back in the 80's. Our fan base rivaled what fans today know about Duke Basketball or Alabama Football. You know that you have a special type of fans when every weekend home game you see students lining up at noon to get into the game that night with their student ID and ticket.

Let's face it, BGSU is never going to compete for national championships in any other sport. The hockey program hasn't had the same type of success in recent decades that was the norm back in the 80's. I struggle to find a sport at BGSU that has a realistic expectation and hope about winning a national championship.

It was great to see the team reach the (first pinnacle) of a season filled with lofty goals. The CCHA win back in the 80's was one of the elite hockey conferences and for an undersized and underfunded program to achieve what it did was a blast.

Who knew then that Coach York would go down in history as one of the greatest college coaches of all time? Who would have known the cast of characters that lead the team who would go onto the NHL from just that roster! Potvin, Duncan, Dahl, Natyshak, Emerson, Barber, Parks, Ysebaert, Flichel and Paluch. Seriously!? Ten!?

I am fortunate that I formed some long-term friendships that exist today. As a roommate for multiple years with Marc Potvin and Kevin Dahl, I got to know all the guys from 86-91 seasons and still keep in contact with many of them.

The fan experience back then was amazing. Picture a fully packed house with that low, "tin cup" ceiling and hearing everyone yell, "Who's he? Nobody!" when the opposing team was introduced. BG Hockey was the ultimate experience for the weekend before heading to Mark's or Brathaus for all kinds of trouble!

Coach York is a L-E-G-E-N-D! How does a coach of a small, "unsexy", university in a location not necessarily known as a "hotbed" of hockey build a program so successful? BG was known to "out-recruit" the legendary schools like Ohio State, University of Michigan, Michigan State, Wisconsin, and many others. The answer is Coach York. He did it his way. Quiet, conservative, respectful of the game, without uttering a word of profanity (that I could ever recall or heard about with my close contacts inside the locker room).

I did not get to know Buddy Powers very well but I know that he was certainly a "player's coach". I would guess that he, along with Terry Flanagan, were the perfect "other side of the coin" to Coach York. Their style was very different than Coach York's and that certainly paid great dividends with the roster that was built to win championships. Buddy and Terry were also outstanding recruiters that delivered both role players and stars!

Remembering Marc Potvin: My memories go very deep with Marc Potvin as he and I grew to become great, lifelong friends. I had the honor of standing up in his wedding and was a pallbearer at his funeral. He had a "bigger than life" personality and he loved his kids and his wife fiercely. He was a guy you wanted at your side if and when you needed a friend. His ridiculously stupid humor was always a welcome addition. The Marc "Herman Munster" Potvin legend lives on to this day!

Greg Parks: Greg was also a classic along the same lines as Marc. A fierce competitor who was incredibly talented but also as loyal of a friend and a teammate that a person could ever ask for.

The most important thing that I took from those years at BGSU were the lifelong friendships that still exist today. Being present for the 40th year celebration of the National Championship really was a joy. It was pure joy to bump into old friends that I had not seen in so many years, but had spent so much time with in the past. You really can identify great relationships when so much time has elapsed and then in an instant, those years all just fade away with a handshake or a hug.

I think legendary boosters/fans like Chuck and Deb Elliot (owners of Wizard Graphics) who have sadly both passed away should get a mention. These two really were the closest things to parents or maybe "uncle and aunt" to so many players who traveled so far to come play at BG. I remember Sunday croquet tournaments and 8-10 players just hanging out, grilling or relaxing or playing with their dog Max. Their very modest house on South Main was a great place to hang out.

Scott Slater was also a great friend and continues to be a constant for the BG hockey program. He had players over at his house for dinner. I remember many nights enjoying a home cooked meal with all of his little kids running around. They viewed us like big brothers and we fully obliged them for a moment in a time. It felt like a home away from home.

Also, Mark Pape (owner of Mark's Pizza Pub..aka "Poppy") or Greg Ralph (manager of Brathaus at the time, aka "J.D.") made the experience of being in BG really special.

From the Photo Album

C.C.H.A Champions!!
1986-87 BGSU Falcon Hockey Team

L To R: Co-Captains Todd Flichel and Iain Duncan
with CCHA Championship Banner
February 21, 1987

Celebration

Todd Flichel and Gary Kruzich celebrate

L to R: Todd Flichel, Tom Pratt, Iain Duncan

Final Buzzer!!

L to R: Greg Parks, Gary Kruzich, Kevin Dahl, Clark Pineo

Team and Fans Celebrate

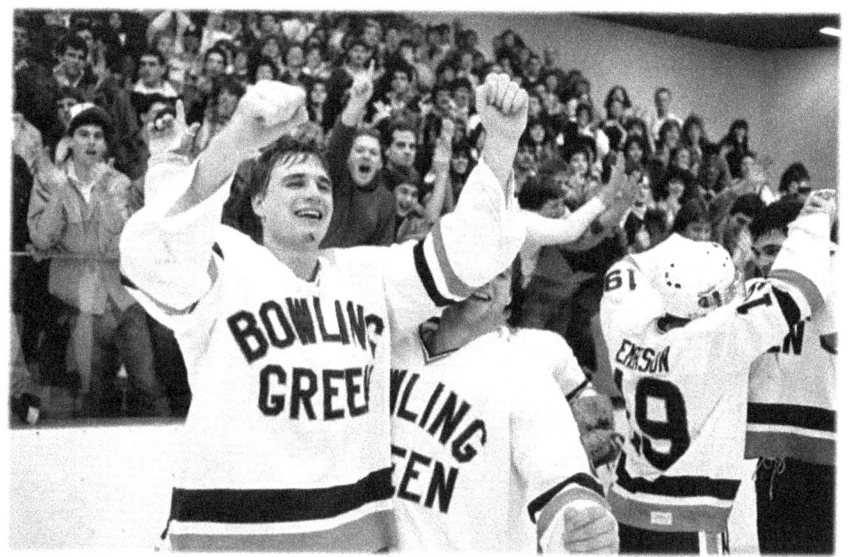
Mike Natyshak celebrates with team and fans

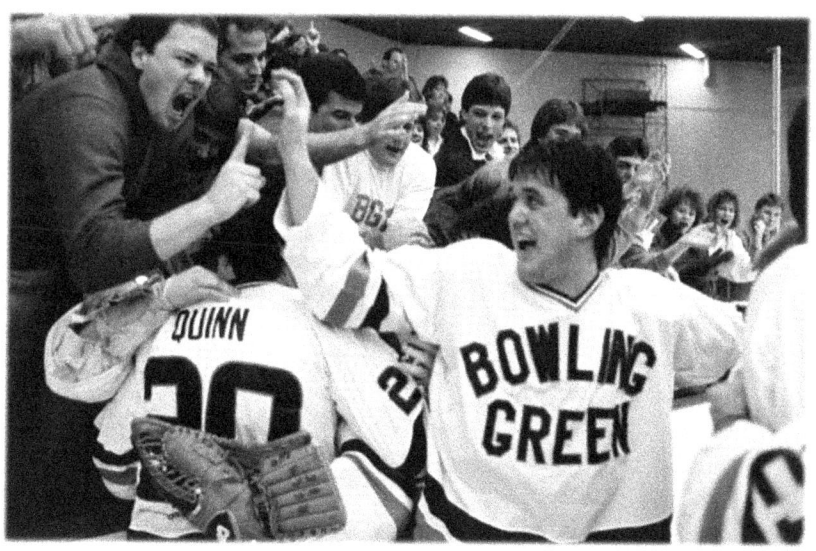
Scott Paluch with fans and teammates

Co-Captains (L to R) Todd Flichel and Iain Duncan

BGSU Falcon Hockey Fans!

This was a visual staple at all of the BGSU home hockey games.

Fans would hold up the newspapers when the opposing team was introduced. After each introduction, fans would shout, "Who's he? Nobody!"

After all of the introductions were announced, fans would crumple up the newspapers and throw them...

*Team Hangout!
Many memories were made and shared at these two beloved establishments!*

Gary Kruzich

Brent Regan, Paul Ysebaert and Scott Paluch

Mark and Maria Potvin

(L to R) Greg Parks with his parents Bonnie & Gordon

Mike Natyshak & Brian McKee

Andy Gribble, Brian Meharry & Don Barber

Wayne Wilson and Kevin Mann

Iain Duncan

Mike Natyshak and Todd Flichel

Coach Terry Flanagan, Wayne Wilson, Kevin Mann

Scott Paluch and Brent Regan

Kevin Dahl

Clarke Pineo

Greg Parks

Andy Gribble, Brent Regan, Scott Paluch and Brian Meharry

Paul Connell and Chad Arthur

Alan Leggett

Tom Pratt

Steve Dickinson

Nelson Emerson and Joe Quinn

Rob Urban and Mike Natyshak

Team Photos and Portraits provided by:

Bowling Green State University Center for Archival Collections

Special Thanks to:
Allison Brandeberr, Athletic Archivist
Jennifer Long Morehart, University Archivist
CAC Student Employees:
Lily Fritsch, Bill Cusack, Paige Pasztor, Sophia Mercer

For more information regarding the archives or to request reprints of photos, please visit:

https://www.bgsu.edu/library/cac.html

or contact:

William T. Jerome Library, 5th Floor
University Libraries
Bowling Green State University
Bowling Green, OH 43403
419-372-2411
archive@bgsu.edu

When requesting reprints of photos, please see the photo index for reference

For more information regarding Bowling Green Hockey, please visit:
https://bgsufalcons.com/sports/mens-ice-hockey

Photo Index

Page	Photo	Archive Reference #/Photo Credit
1	Jerry York & Terry Flanagan	Ref# ua00026b-0002
2	Jerry York, Portrait	Ref# ua00026b-0001
5	Buddy Powers, Portrait	Ref# ua00026b-00001
9	Wayne Wilson, Portrait	Ref# ua00026b-00001
12	Kevin Mann, Portrait	Ref# bgsu-0932-0046
15	Players Line-up	*Personal collection of LeeAnn Rasey*
16	Paul Connell, Portrait	Ref# BGSU-0917-0069-0003
16	Paul Connell, Uniform	Ref# BGSU 0917-0069-0004
17	Paul Connell, Action 1	Ref# BGSU-0917-0069-0001
17	Paul Connell, Action 2	Ref# BGSU-0917-0069-0002
22	Tom Pratt, Portrait	Ref# BGSU-0971-0044-0003
22	Tom Pratt, Uniform	Ref# BGSU-0971-0044-0004
23	Tom Pratt, Action 1	Ref# BGSU-0971-0044-0001
23	Tom Pratt, Action 2	Ref# BGSU-0971-0044-0002
26	Todd Flichel, Portrait	Ref# BGSU0928-0055-0004
26	Todd Flichel, Uniform	Ref# BGSU-0928-0055-0003
27	Todd Flichel, Action 1	Ref# BGSU-0928-0055-0001
27	Todd Flichel, Action 2	Ref# BGSU-0928-0055-0002
31	Scott Paluch, Portrait	Ref# BGSU-0967-0044-0003
31	Scott Paluch, Uniform	Ref# BGSU-0967-0044-0004
32	Scott Paluch, Action 1	Ref# BGSU-0967-0044-0002
32	Scott Paluch, Action 2	Ref# BGSU-0967-0044-0001
35	Kevin Dahl, Portrait	Ref# BGSU-0919-0061-0003
35	Kevin Dahl, Uniform	Ref# BGSU-0919-0061-0004
36	Kevin Dahl, Action 1	Ref# BGSU-0919-0061-0001
36	Kevin Dahl, Action 2	Ref# BGSU-0929-0061-0002
39	Thad Rusiecki, Portrait	Ref# BGSU-0977-0018-0004
39	Thad Rusiecki, Uniform	Ref# BGSU-0977-0018-0003
40	Thad Rusiecki, Action 1	Ref# BGSU-0977-0018-0001
40	Thad Rusiecki, Action 2	Ref# BGSU-0977-0018-0002
43	Brian McKee, Portrait	Ref#BGSU-0958-0041-0003
43	Brian McKee, Uniform	Ref#BGSU-0958-0041-0004
44	Brian McKee, Action 1	Ref#BGSU-0958-0041-0001
44	Brian McKee, Action 2	Ref#BGSU-0958-0041-0001
47	Alan Leggett, Portrait	Ref#BGSU-0957-0057-0004

47	Alan Leggett, Uniform	Ref#BGSU-0957-0057-0003
48	Alan Leggett, Action 1	Ref#BGSU-0957-0057-0001
48	Alan Leggett, Action 2	Ref#BGSU-0957-0057-0002
51	Rob Urban, Portrait	Ref#BGSU-0990-0052-0002
51	Rob Urban, Uniform	Ref#GSU-0990-0052-0001
52	Rob Urban, Action 1	Ref#BGSU-0990-0052-0003
52	Rob Urban, Action 2	Ref#BGSU-0990-0052-0004
57	Paul Ysebaert, Portrait	Ref#BGSU-0998-0044-0003
57	Paul Ysebaert, Uniform	Ref#BGSU-0998-0044-0004
58	Paul Ysebaert, Action 1	Ref#BGSU-0998-0044-0002
58	Paul Ysebaert, Action 2	Ref#BGSU-0998-0044-0001
61	Mark Lori, Portrait	Ref#BGSU-0093-0057-0003
61	Mark Lori, Uniform	Ref#BGSU-0093-0002
62	Mark Lori, Action 1	Ref#BGSU-0953-0057-0001
62	Mark Lori, Action 2	Ref#BGSU-0953-0057-0004
65	Andy Gribble, Portrait	Ref#BGSU-0933-0028-0003
65	Andy Gribble, Uniform	Ref#BGSU-0933-0028-0004
66	Andy Gribble, Action 1	Ref#BGSU-0933-0028-0001
66	Andy Gribble, Action 2	Ref#BGSU-0933-0028-0002
69	Marc Potvin, Portrait	Ref#BGSU-0971-0030-0001
69	Marc Potvin, Uniform	Ref#BGSU-0971-0030-0002
70	Marc Potvin, Action 1	Ref#BGSU-0971-0030-0003
70	Marc Potvin, Action 2	Ref#BGSU-0971-0030-0004
72	Greg Parks, Portrait	Ref#BGSU-0968-0012-0004
72	Greg Parks, Uniform	Ref#BGSU-0969-0012-0003
73	Greg Parks, Action 1	Ref#BGSU-0968-0012-0001
73	Greg Parks, Action 2	Ref#BGSU-0968-0002
76	Don Barber, Portrait	Ref#BGSU-0905-0051-0002
76	Don Barber, Uniform	Ref#BGSU-0905-0051-0001
76	Don Barber, Action 1	Ref#BGSU-0905-0051-0003
76	Don Barber, Action 2	Ref#BGSU-0905-0051-0004
77	Geoff Williams, Portrait	Ref#BGSU-0995-0061-0002
77	Geoff Williams, Uniform	Ref#BGSU-0995-0061-0001
77	Geoff Williams, Action 1	Ref#BGSU-0995-0061-0003
77	Geoff Williams, Action 2	Ref#BGSU-0095-0061-0004
78	Brent Regan, Portrait	Ref#BGSU-0973-0064-0004
78	Brent Regan, Uniform	Ref#BGSU-0973-0064-0003
79	Brent Regan, Action 1	Ref#BGSU-0973-0064-0001
79	Brent Regan, Action 2	Ref#BGSU-0973-0064-0002
82	Nelson Emerson, Portrait	Ref#ua00037-ns86-s0475-f00016

82	Nelson Emerson, Uniform	Ref#ua37-ns86-s0646-f00014
83	Nelson Emerson, Action 1	Ref#BGSU-0926-0006-0001
83	Nelson Emerson, Action 2	Ref#BGSU-0926-0006-0002
87	Joe Quinn, Portrait	Ref#BGSU-0972-0043-0004
87	Joe Quinn, Uniform	Ref#BGSU-0972-0043-0003
88	Joe Quinn, Action 1	Ref#BGSU-00972-0043-0001
88	Joe Quinn, Action 2	Ref#BGSU-00972-0002
92	Clarke Pineo, Portrait	Ref#BGSU-0970-0023-0004
92	Clarke Pineo, Uniform	Ref#BGSU-0970-0023-0003
93	Clarke Pineo, Action 1	Ref#BGSU-0970-0023-0001
93	Clarke Pineo, Action 2	Ref#BGSU-0970-0023-0002
96	Brian Meharry, Portrait	Ref#BGSU-0959-0047-0003
96	Brian Meharry, Uniform	Ref#BGSU-0959-0047-0004
97	Brian Meharry, Action 1	Ref#BGSU-0959-0047-0001
97	Brian Meharry, Action 2	Ref#BGSU-0959-0047-0002
101	Chad Arthur, Portrait	Ref#BGSU-0903-0056-0001
101	Chad Arthur, Uniform	Ref#BGSU-0903-0056-0002
102	Chad Arthur, Action 1	Ref#BGSU-0903-0056-0003
102	Chad Arthur, Action 2	Ref#BGSU-0903-0056-0004
105	Iain Duncan, Portrait	Ref#BGSU-0924-0009-0002
105	Iain Duncan, Uniform	Ref#BGSU-0924-0009-0001
106	Iain Duncan, Action 1	Ref#BGSU-0924-0009-0004
106	Iain Duncan, Action 2	Ref#BGSU-0924-0009-0003
110	Steve Dickinson, Portrait	Ref#BGSU-0922-0050-0001
110	Steve Dickinson, Uniform	Ref#BGSU-0922-0050-0002
111	Steve Dickinson, Action 1	Ref#BGSU-0922-0050-0003
111	Steve Dickinson, Action 2	Ref#BGSU-0922-0050-0004
114	Mike Natyshak, Portrait	Ref#BGSU-0964-0025-0004
114	Mike Natyshak, Uniform	Ref#BGSU-0964-0025-0003
115	Mike Natyshak, Action 1	Ref#BGSU-0964-0025-0002
115	Mike Natyshak, Action 2	Ref#BGSU-0964-0025-0001
119	Dan Kwilas, Portrait	Ref#BGSU-0949-0074-0003
119	Dan Kwilas, Uniform	Ref#BGSU-0949-0074-0004
119	Dan Kwilas, Action 1	Ref#BGSU-0949-0074-0001
119	Dan Kwilas, Action 2	Ref#BGSU-0949-0074-0002
120	Gary Kruzich, Portrait	Ref#BGSU-0949-0042-0004
120	Gary Kruzich, Uniform	Ref#BGSU-0949-0042-0003
121	Gary Kruzich, Action 1	Ref#BGSU-0949-0042-0002
121	Gary Kruzich, Action 2	Ref#BGSU-0949-0042-0001
128	Dr. Tom Wojciechowski	Ref#BGSU-0924-0009-0003

133	Don "Woody" Woods	*Kristen Woods-Batcho*
133	Gum Ball Machine	*Kristen Woods-Batcho*
139	Jeff Shell	*Personal collection*
144	Frieda Falcon	*Rhonda Albers*
144	Frieda Falcon	*Rhonda Albers*
151	Dave Shilling and Rhonda Albers	*Dave Shilling*
152	Dave Kuhar	*Personal collection*
155	Todd Parker	Ref#0018
166	CCHA Championship Banner	Ref#BGSU-11-18
166	Banner Co-Captains	Ref#BGSU-0544-0001-0009
167	Todd Flichel and Gary Kruzich	Ref#BGSU-2781
167	Championship Ring	*Personal collection*
167	Championship Trophy	Ref #20240422_155517
167	Flichel, Pratt, Duncan	Ref#ua00037-ns86-s2024-f00009
168	Parks, Kruzich, Dahl, Pineo	Ref#ua00037-ns86-2026-f000020
168	Team and Fans Celebrate	Ref#0018
169	Mike Natyshak	Ref#ua00037-ns86-2025-f00019
169	Scott Paluch	Ref#ua00037-ns86-2025-f00016
170	Todd Flichel and Iain Duncan	Ref#ua00037-ns86-c0827-00002
171	Newspaper Fans	Ref#BGSU-0544-0001-0024
172	Mark's Pizza Pub	*Personal collection*
172	Brathaus	*Personal collection*
173	Gary Kruzich	*Angela Gorgone Swartz*
173	Regan, Ysebaert, and Paluch	*Paul Ysebaert*
174	Mark and Maria Potvin	*Maria Potvin*
174	Greg Parks Family Photo	*Bonnie Parks*
175	Natyshak and McKee	*Angela Gorgone Swartz*
175	Gribble, Meharry, and Barber	*Angela Gorgone Swartz*
176	Wayne Wilson and Kevin Mann	*Angela Gorgone Swartz*
176	Iain Duncan	*Angela Gorgone Swartz*
176	Mike Natyshak and Todd Flichel	*Angela Gorgone Swartz*
177	Flanagan, Wilson Mann	*Angela Gorgone Swartz*
177	Scott Paluch and Brian Regan	*Angela Gorgone Swartz*
178	Kevin Dahl	*Angela Gorgone Swartz*
178	Clarke Pineo	*Angela Gorgone Swartz*
178	Greg Parks	*Angela Gorgone Swartz*
179	Gribble, Regan Paluch, & Meharry	*Angela Gorgone Swartz*
179	Paul Connel and Chad Arthur	*Angela Gorgone Swartz*
180	Alan Leggett	*Angela Gorgone Swartz*
180	Tom Pratt	*Angela Gorgone Swartz*

180	Steve Dickinson	*Angela Gorgone Swartz*
181	Rob Urban and Mike Natyshak	*Angela Gorgone Swartz*
181	Nelson Emerson and Joe Quinn	*Angela Gorgone Swartz*

Helen Rose Marketti

Helen Marketti has been a freelance writer for 17 years. She is a music and entertainment columnist for Lifestyles Magazine (Fremont, OH) and the North Coast Voice Magazine (Cleveland, OH). Her first book, "The Long & Winding Phone" (Blue Jade Press, 2024) is a collection of "Beatles-related" interviews.

Helen is also a big hockey fan! She became a hockey fan while attending Bowling Green State University during the 80s! Her recent book, "Skill, Size, Strength & Speed" The 1986-87 BGSU Falcon Hockey Team (Blue Jade Press, 2025) is a collection of 50 interviews with former coaching staff, players, support staff, family, friends and fans. The book primarily focuses on the Central Collegiate Hockey Association (CCHA) title win on Saturday, February 21, 1987.

This book is a time capsule of that era and those who were there and witnessed another outstanding time in Bowling Green's hockey history. It is a must read for hockey fans, sports enthusiasts and young men and women who aspire to play hockey at any level. Former players from the 1986-87 season provide insight and advice in addition to reliving their own memories while playing at BG.

These pages are about a hockey team that was electrifying to watch, fans that rattled the opponents and loved their Falcons, plus a community that showed their support at each and every game.

Helen R. Marketti
1988 BGSU Graduate
Bachelor of Science in Elementary Education

www.helenrosemarketti.com
Email: helenwheels465@gmail.com

Books may be purchased through contacting Helen directly who will be happy to autograph your copy. You may also purchase copies through Amazon.

www.ingramcontent.com/pod-product-compliance
Lightning Source LLC
Chambersburg PA
CBHW071201160426
43196CB00011B/2150